The Dynamics of

Spiritual
Formation

Other books in the
Ministry Dynamics for a New Century series
WARREN W. WIERSBE, series editor

The Dynamics of
Spiritual
Formation

MEL LAWRENZ

Baker Books

A Division of Baker Book House Co
Grand Rapids, Michigan 49516

© 2000 by Mel Lawrenz

Published by Baker Books
a division of Baker Book House Company
P.O. Box 6287, Grand Rapids, MI 49516-6287

Printed in the United States of America

Library of Congress Cataloging-in-Publication Data

Lawrenz, Mel.
    The dynamics of spiritual formation / Mel Lawrenz.
       p. cm.—(Ministry dynamics for a new century)
    Includes bibliographical references and index.
    ISBN 0-8010-9097-0 (pbk.)
       1. Spiritual formation.   I. Title.   II. Series.
    BV4501.2.L364 2000
    253.5′3—dc21   99–055497

For current information about all releases from Baker Book House, visit our web site:

http://www.bakerbooks.com

To my mother, Arlene Lawrenz

Contents

Series Preface

The purpose of the Ministry Dynamics series is to provide both experienced and beginning pastors with concise information that will help them do the task of ministry with efficiency, fruitfulness, and joy.

The word *ministry* means "service," something that Jesus exemplified in his own life and that he expects us to practice in our lives. No matter what our title or position, we are in the church to serve God's people. The word *dynamics* is not used as an equivalent of "power" but as a reminder that nothing stands still in Christian ministry. If it does, it dies. True biblical ministry involves constant challenge and change, learning and growth, and how we handle these various elements determines the strength and success of the work that we do.

The emphasis in this series is on practical service founded on basic principles and not on passing fads. Some older ministers need to catch up with the present while newer ministers need to catch up on the past. We all can learn much from each other if only we're honest enough to admit it and humble enough to accept each other's counsel.

I began pastoring in 1950 and over the years have seen many changes take place in local church ministry, from bus ministries and house churches to growth groups and megachurches. Some of the changes have been good and are now integrated into God's work in many churches. But some ideas that attracted national attention decades ago now exist only on the pages of forgotten books in used-book stores. How quickly today's exciting headlines become tomorrow's footnotes! "Test everything. Hold on to the good" (1 Thess. 5:21).

An ancient anonymous prayer comes to mind:

From the cowardice that shrinks from new truth,
From the laziness that is content with half-truths,
From the arrogance that thinks it knows all truth,
    O God of truth, deliver us!

Our desire is that both the seasoned servant and the new seminary graduate will find encouragement and enlightenment from the Ministry Dynamics series.

Warren W. Wiersbe

Preface

Anyone with any sense of purpose in life will hope that he or she may make a difference, somewhere, somehow. The prospect of the Christian ministry is that, by God's enabling, we will actually have a hand in the formation of persons. What an incredible notion!

"We are being transformed" is what the apostle Paul claims in 2 Corinthians 3:18. And the ministry of the church is nothing less than the business of soul-shaping—though people attending church rarely seek so much and we frequently settle for offering far less. Spiritual growth is not the easy road.

Spirituality is not subjectivism shaking off reason like a wild horse throws its rider; nor is it like a bridled, tired, old mare. Spiritual leaders are called to lead people (and to be led) into a mode of living that is decidedly ordinary (because all people are spiritual creatures) yet notably uncommon (because humans so easily acquiesce to the gravity of fallenness). As such, spiritual formation is not elitist, nor is it run-of-the-mill. Its motive is not to produce a spiritual stratification of church members, but to respond appropriately to each person's level of readiness for growth.

In the end, the best Christian leaders can aspire to is to be able to step back from the work and confess, "God made it grow." We must echo Paul's assessment: "What, after all, is Apollos? And what is Paul? Only servants, through whom you came to believe—as the Lord has assigned to each his task. I planted the seed, Apollos watered it, but God made it grow. So neither he who plants nor he who waters is anything, but only God, who makes things grow" (1 Cor. 3:5–7).

Today there are many good books about personal spiritual growth, and in recent years practical books about ministry in the local church have flourished. This book will try to bridge the gap between these issues—to bring principles of personal formation and corporate church life together by addressing important questions: How do typical church activities (worship, prayer, fellowship, etc.) contribute to the spiritual formation of its members? What makes the difference between going through the motions and accomplishing actual transformation? How do we aim at people's souls? How can the church make contact with the innermost lives of its members?

The task of shepherding the church belongs not only to those engaged in full-time ministry, but a multitude of others as well. So the topics in this book are the domain of anyone involved in shepherding the local church: pastors, other ministry staff members, lay leaders, Bible teachers, and others.

For my part, I am enthused about contributing to this series on ministry in a new century. After more than twenty years of pastoral ministry in rural and urban, denominational and nondenominational churches, I am continually amazed at the commonality of our pursuit—the cure of souls. This pursuit is not at all new, yet in every way new as each passing generation takes fresh approaches to ministry. The trajectory of the church into the future is as reliable as our understanding of our past. The most valuable insights in this book have already stood the test of time.

> My God, grant me the conversion of my parish; I am willing to suffer all my life whatsoever it may please thee to lay upon me; yes even for a hundred years am I prepared to endure the sharpest pains, only let my people be converted.
>
> Curé d'Ars (1786–1859)

The Formed Life

Spiritual Growth as Spiritual Formation

> Lord, when my eye confronts my heart, and I realize that you have filled my heart with your love, I am breathless with amazement. Once my heart was so small in its vision, so narrow in its compassion, so weak in its zeal for truth. Then you chose to enter my heart, and now in my heart I can see you, I can love all your people, and I have courage to proclaim the truth of your gospel to anyone and everyone. Like wax before a fire, my heart has melted under the heat of your love.
>
> Count von Zinzendorf (1700–1760)

Growth and Form

Spiritual formation is the progressive patterning of a person's inner and outer life according to the image of Christ through intentional means of spiritual growth.

It is neither a novel concept nor one limited to any particular tradition. Its biblical foundation is in the idea that God creates with form, and in a broken world, his work of salvation is best called trans*form*ation. The mission of the church in making disciples is to provide the means whereby fractured and misshapen lives can be re-*formed* according to the pattern of the perfect man, Jesus Christ. We are to be con*formed* to him, not to the world. Disciples of Jesus are those who are continually being reshaped in thought, word, and deed. Spiritual growth, as is the case with any kind of healthy growth, follows a certain form. It is not random, accidental, or arbitrary.

Growth without form or structure is what happens with cancer—millions of cells that have escaped the normal forces regulating cell growth expand and divide, producing more tissue, but more corruption. Eventually a *growth* is discovered. But because it has not been formed according to the body's design, it represents sickness rather than health.

The Christian centuries have seen numerous instances of growth without form. Heresies erupt and cults emerge when spiritual renewal occurs without formative teaching and disciplines.

Form without growth can be just as deathly. Paul's warning about those who hold to "a *form* of godliness but deny its power" (2 Tim. 3:5) foreshadows chapters in church history when our fallen nature has tempted us to hold to the form of religion while ignoring spiritual vitality. Impressive religious form echoes with the hollowness of an abandoned ruin in the absence of spiritual growth. Such a path is strewn with mindless prayers, mechanical Bible studies, and impressive edifices that kill real spiritual life when they are married to a motive of perfunctory spirituality. It is tame religion that anyone with even a little time and energy can handle—a religion that is sure not to bite you back. It appeals to rebellious human nature as a system of pleasing God with little cost or intrusiveness. A few become vocational practitioners, and the rest merely practice the mechanics of the discipline. No one gets hurt, and no one is really changed.

If growth means anything, though, it means change. And formative growth requires constructive change. Scripture frequently uses biological metaphors to help us understand spiritual growth. The Word of God is "seed"; the kingdom of God is a "harvest"; the world is a "field."

We see formative growth in trees, which is why we don't stroll among sixty-foot acorns. Babies grow into adults, being formed and changed along the way. Otherwise a six-foot man would have a head the size of an auto tire. The embryo of a human and that of a fish look almost identical, but the DNA in every cell determines that one will grow into an Asian woman five feet tall and the other into a male carp with a white patch on one side of its dorsal fin. Microscopic divine instructions dictate development: Buds on an embryo turn into arms and legs; specks become eyes that work in stereo to process light, shadow, and distance; and blobs of tissue become muscle, sinew, and bone. And what comes of it all may turn out to be a first baseman or a surgeon—in every case an individual able to take that formed growth and use it to the glory of God.

All good growth is formed growth. And the form's design must come from God. God stipulated this principle early on in history: "You shall not make for yourself an idol in the *form* of anything in heaven above or on the earth beneath or in the waters below" (Exod. 20:4). How we love what our hands shape, and how quick we are to adore the fabricated over the created! But God has taught us repeatedly that he is the sole designer of spiritual endeavors. Take the lesson of the temple: God defined the form of the temple; God gave the craftsmen the skill to construct it; and God dictated that all the chiseling be done at the quarry so that the temple would rise in holy quietness from the threshing floor of Araunah. Likewise, spiritual growth can only come from God and by his design.

Spiritual Growth and Soul-Shaping

Most Christian leaders will on occasion stop in their tracks to ask, "Now just what was it we were supposed to be doing here? What really is the purpose of the church?" The easy (and entirely correct) answer is that we are to make disciples. We understand this imperative of Jesus to mean helping people come to and grow in faith. But how does one measure whether spiritual growth is happening? Is it the number of home Bible studies in the church? The number of members? The giving? How do we know there is spiritual growth happening in this place at all—that we are not just going through the motions?

A young John Wesley found himself asking a similar question. An ordained Anglican priest, a missionary to the Indians in Georgia, and a discipline-lover so inclined to spiritual methodology that he and his friends were called Bible Moths and Methodists, Wesley realized in 1738 that he had no assurance that Christ had saved him.

Back in England Wesley and his fellow members of "the Holy Club" had constructed an impressive spiritual discipline—frequent communion; fasting two days a week; intensive study; distribution of food, clothing, medicine, and books; and visiting prisoners and helping to reform their lives. But Wesley heard no applause from heaven. He could not understand why the Georgian Indians didn't welcome his disciplines with open hearts, and he antagonized his flock with high churchmanship. When he was spurned by Sophia Hopkey, the niece of the local magistrate, he used his spirituality as a weapon to exclude her from communion.

Wesley the cleric began to become Wesley the pastor the day God began to form him spiritually in the deep places for the first time in his life. A heart "strangely warmed" became a heart alive to the shaping influence of the Spirit of God rather than a heart chiseled by his own hand.

So what exactly is it we are supposed to be doing here? If we neither give cursory answers to nor become paralyzed by this question, it will remind us just how marvelous, preposterous, and mysterious is this thing called shepherding. It is, in short, the business of soul-shaping. As such, it is not a job invented by a corporation, nor is it an entrepreneurial adventure. It cannot be anything other than a calling. For who would be so absurd as to set out to shape the souls of other people?

The tools for soul-shaping have not changed since the apostolic age. *Preaching and teaching* grant us entry into people's lives at the core of their being—where decisions are made, values are shaped, ideas are borne, passions are ignited, wounds are soothed, hardness is broken. The intense ministry of *pastoral counseling* finds one soul speaking in sanctified confidence to another, and one (or both) being better shaped. In *worship* a community of spiritual beings participate in a planned encounter with the Spirit who is their maker. The ministry of *prayer* extends from Jesus' teaching for his disciples when they requested, "Teach us to pray." Well-taught prayer is spirit-to-Spirit communication, a divine dialogue which cannot help but shape the souls of those who engage it. Developing *fellowship,* one of the essentials of ministry, links people to each other and facilitates soul-shaping through accountability and sup-

port. Leading people to *service* is to put them at the ful-
crum where earthly stress and divine grace meet, where
their hearts might be broken, then made stronger.

These are not tired old habits or quaint repetitions
of bygone churchiness. They endure as the time-honored shepherding disciplines that aim people at the
kingdom of God.

In ministry we also teach people how to position
their lives so that there is opportunity for these disciplines to work. How do we tune out the noise of the
world so we can hear God speaking? How do we get
out of the bondage of busyness, not to land in laziness,
but to be exercised by God? What attitudes will keep
our hearts and minds open to the shaping influence
of the Spirit, and what ones will extinguish the Spirit?

The Principles of Spiritual Formation

Many biblical passages can serve as touchstones for
the ministry of spiritual formation, but one that is
surely among the most helpful is Paul's statement in
Ephesians 4:

> It was he who gave some to be apostles, some
> to be prophets, some to be evangelists, and some
> to be pastors and teachers, to prepare God's peo-
> ple for works of service, so that the body of Christ
> may be built up until we all reach unity in the faith
> and in the knowledge of the Son of God and
> become mature, attaining to the whole measure
> of the fullness of Christ. . . . Speaking the truth
> in love, we will in all things grow up into him who
> is the Head, that is, Christ. From him the whole
> body, joined and held together by every sup-
> porting ligament, grows and builds itself up in
> love, as each part does its work.
>
> verses 11–13, 15–16

Notice many of the oft-repeated keywords of spiritual life—Christ, love, truth, knowledge, work—but also notice some of the principles brought together here:

the final goal of spiritual life—"attaining to the whole measure of *the fullness of Christ*"

the intermediate goal of spiritual life—"reach[ing] unity in the faith and in the knowledge of the Son of God"

the process of spiritual life—"grow[ing] up into . . . Christ"

spiritual formation as communal and constructive—"that the *body* of Christ may be *built* up"

the labor of spiritual life—"works of service"

the ministers of spiritual life—"pastors and teachers"

To come back to the case of John Wesley, there were several key things that happened in 1738, his year of change, that God used to remove Wesley's shell of religion and to make him into a real pastor. First, Wesley came face-to-face with his spiritual impoverishment. Observing the contentment and assurance on the faces of some Moravian missionaries during a stormy Atlantic crossing made Wesley realize that he had no such peace. He was shaken by this realization as well as by his failure as a missionary in Georgia. Second, he experienced genuine brotherhood among the Moravians back in London and came under the formative influence of Moravian leader Peter Böhler. Third, he encountered the sharp, discerning edge of God's Word when at a Bible meeting he heard the account of Martin Luther's discovery of justification by grace through faith. Through jarring encounters—with his poverty, with a live community of believers, with a mentor, and with

God's Word—living growth was added to form that was already there, and a world-changing leader was born.

Wesley's transformation took place during an age of spiritual renewal that developed into a movement that would force the issue of growth and form in the lives of many people. During the Great Awakening in America old forms of Christianity met the fresh winds of spiritual revival, and people came to faith in large numbers. In a clash between form and growth, "old lights" (those threatened by the renewal) rejected the new growth while some "new lights" (those wrapped up in the renewal) sometimes rejected form. What emerged after the struggle were people and churches who welcomed both growth and form, and who passed on genuine spiritual life to the next generation.

Foundational to this book are some basic principles regarding spiritual formation:

1. Spiritual formation has not been developed in a late chapter of Christian history or by any particular group. It is as old as Christian faith itself.
2. Spiritual formation must be part of the normal Christian life, not the domain of an elite few.
3. God uses diverse means—including the Word, the Christian community, and personal disciplines—to form us spiritually.
4. God has promoted diverse disciplines such as prayer and meditation, Scripture reading, worship, and service, in the interest of spiritual formation.
5. Spiritual formation depends on the attitude and disposition of the believer.
6. Spiritual formation is intensely personal, but it is not isolated from the Christian community.
7. Christian communities can choose to provide a conducive atmosphere and promote appropriate values for spiritual formation.

In recent times churches have gotten wonderfully adept at forming their organization and programs. It should come as no wonder that people in the churches long for and ask for more than well-oiled machines. They say to their leaders: Please fill our souls.

Taking Aim at the Soul

In ministry we must take aim at the *heart* of human experience, the matters of the soul. We should avoid the temptation to be caught up with peripheral issues.

When we look out at a congregation we can choose to focus on the differences that are so apparent. There is Mr. Johnson who just turned eighty; Mrs. Wilson who just discovered fast-growing, life-threatening skin cancer; Joseph, the exchange student from Paraguay; Mary Ann, the high school freshman; Scott, the computer technician by day, church drama director by weekend; and so the list continues. We're looking out at only a small splash of the sea of humanity, but even this relatively small group shows the incredible diversity of human soul and body. So, at what do we aim? Do we try to understand all the nuances of every person's distinct life experience?

We should try to understand as much as possible because shepherds are supposed to know their sheep. But if we are honest, we know that there really isn't any way to comprehend the special and varied life experiences of all those people. Though sociologists have to do it, it's questionable whether Christian leaders should look at people under the rubric of the social categories into which they fit. When it comes to fundamental fears, hopes, sin, and spiritual needs, the twenty-five-year-old isn't all that different from the eighty-year-old. The basic state of the human soul is a remarkably constant phenomenon for all places and all times. If every human being were a watch, the list of parts inside would be the same for Julius Caesar, Marilyn Monroe, Billy Graham, an African rural farmer, an Asian factory worker, FDR, and your teenage daughter.

The realm of the soul is a wide expanse in which we find a substantial commonality. The truly important questions of life, those that really matter for the course of a lifetime and that we long to have answered, are basically the same for all people regardless of age, social rank, or place in the world.

Why am I here?

Is there a God? If so, what is he like?

What has gone wrong in the world?

What is wrong in me?

How can I be rescued from myself and from those who would wrong me?

What should I be doing with my time and energy?

How can I make sense of the present?

Where do I belong?

Am I alone?

Where is God when I am suffering?

Why am I afraid?

What should I do with my guilt?

What am I supposed to have learned from the past?

What should I believe? (the question of faith)

What is going to happen to me in the future? (the question of hope)

Does anyone care about me? (the question of love)

These questions prompt hundreds of others, and they represent the issues that the Scriptures come back to again and again. They are, as the hymn says, "the hopes and fears of all the years" and of all generations and all nationalities. They represent the common ground of humanity—the realm of the soul which is the center of the field of ministry.

Some believe that the key to ministry is to understand the differences between people and to aim in that direction. That view assumes that the human center is not common ground.

If, however, we believe that the spiritual center of all human beings is common ground, then we can trust that preaching, fellowship, worship, and any other form of ministry that aims at this core, will address the things that matter most to people. We will see people experience the gospel of Christ, we will enjoy many occasions for the diverse church to come together, and we will maintain a distinctly spiritual mission. We will always need to adjust our communication to different groups

Figure 1
Little Common Ground = Ministry Aimed at Periphery

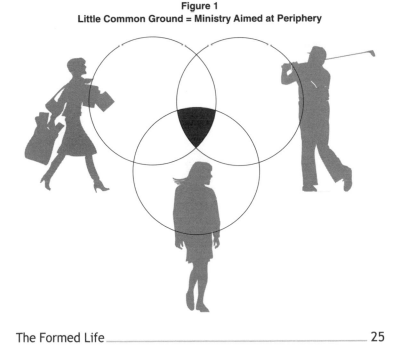

based on the language they use, but we can always aim at the soul, believing that connections are made at the core rather than the edges of human nature.

Indeed, it doesn't make sense for us to aim at anything other than the center when we do ministry. An archer always aims at the bull's-eye. A quarterback always aims at the numbers on the jersey. And although we could spend years in ministry aimed at the soul without finishing the work, ministry that strikes anywhere near that center produces reaction and response.

Figure 2
Large Common Ground = Ministry Aimed at the Soul

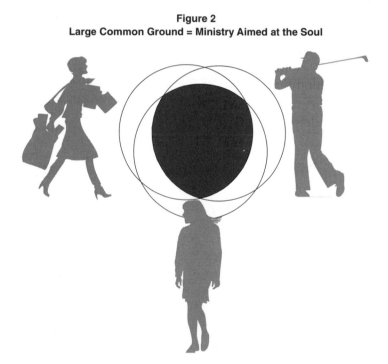

Types of Christian Spiritual Experience

How should we understand the conspicuous differences between Christians in their approach to spiritual

The Dynamics of Spiritual Formation

life? There is no question that issues of temperament and past experience as well as philosophy and theology influence our approach. The chart below describes four types of Christian spiritual experience and their respective emphases.

Emphases of Types of Christian Spirituality

The Activist Approach	The Contemplative Approach
action	quietism
engagement	withdrawal
visibility	hiddenness
pursuing God as holy	pursuing God as love

The Intellectual Approach	The Mystical Approach
intelligibility	ineffability
analysis	intuition
activity	passivity
pursuing God as truth	pursuing God as one

Chances are we will identify with one of these approaches. In fact, we may see ourselves in more than one, for these clearly are not watertight categories. Some will be skeptical of one or more of these emphases, but most Christians will see most of these emphases as having some valid basis in biblical Christianity.

Let's be honest at this point. We all know that intellectual Christians tend to be critical of those who emphasize spiritual intuition (and vice versa), that the activists get frustrated with the contemplatives and the contemplatives wonder whether the activists ever stop to appreciate God for who he is. Some believers invest great energy in categorizing intelligible theological propositions and others understand theology in terms of a love relationship with God.

Is the answer to such tensions to be found in targeting the middle of this grid, aiming one's spiritual life at a perfect middle so that one can be called an activist-contemplative-intellectual-mystical believer, or is the balance to be found in the variations inherent in the believing community? Or is there another alternative—that we accept the inevitability of diverse spiritual dispositions in the body of Christ but also urge individual believers to round out their spiritual experiences by learning from those of others? This approach will allow the intellectually-inclined believer, for instance, to have an appreciation for the contemplative believer and to learn something from him or her. In fact, most mature believers who reflect on the development of their faith will say that there were stages where they realized they needed to redress an imbalance in their approach to spiritual life. They will recall making transitions without falling into the disaster they may have earlier feared.

Whatever one's spiritual temperament, the basic facts are constant: We are dead in sin, rebirth by the Spirit of God is the only path to spiritual life, and that life must develop in a lifelong process of growth, integration, and transformation.

Beyond Birth

The Development of Spiritual Life

> O Son of God, perform a miracle for me; change my heart. You, whose crimson blood redeems mankind, whiten my heart. It is you who makes the sun bright and the ice sparkle; you who makes the rivers flow and the salmon leap. Your skilled hand makes the nut tree blossom, and the corn turn golden; your spirit composes the songs of the birds and the buzz of the bees. Your creation is a million wondrous miracles, beautiful to behold. I ask of you just one more miracle: beautify my soul.
>
> Celtic prayer

God grows what he makes.

Birth, that miracle of beginning, is the prelude to the ongoing, creative act of God that we call growth. Often we focus on the immediate event rather than the ongoing process. Bride and groom sometimes focus more on the wedding than on the marriage, and young parents sometimes spend more time preparing the nursery than preparing to raise a child to adulthood. Likewise, in the church we sometimes speak more about spiritual beginnings than about the challenging, complex process of spiritual growth and formation. And that shouldn't surprise us. Birth is a boisterous climax of pain and joy. It is an arrival and a revelation. It's easy to talk about and natural to celebrate.

The joy in the delivery room, however, is nothing compared to the drama of being spiritually reborn. Jesus shocked Nicodemus with the notion (John 3). In Jesus' parable of the prodigal, the father says, "This son of mine was dead and is alive again." And so it goes through the New Testament. Spiritual birth means an awakening to God based on a new relationship with God that is so radical that it is called the difference between death and life.

Growth, on the other hand, doesn't always seem as exciting. It's often painfully slow—with a few leaps and bounds, but also long interludes and sometimes even regression. Some believers seem to not want growth, and others prematurely claim a spiritual status that is more wishful thinking than reality. Yet this is God's chosen way, and we must understand it.

It takes courage to really long for spiritual growth in the people you minister to or in yourself. We will have a healthy sense that we've gotten into more than what we bargained for. It's not easy to deal with disappointing results. It's hard to know just how much to expect and how soon. Yet not to go out on a limb and have a passion for spiritual growth is to risk settling for the status quo or to acquiesce to the world, the flesh, and the devil.

Spiritual Development as Growth

The idea of growth comes from the world of nature. The word itself is related to green and grass in Old

English. The New Testament is full of the idea of growth. Jesus used many agricultural metaphors: the sower going out to sow, the farmer caring for his field, the cropmaster looking to maximize his yield, the harvester winnowing the grain. These and other pictures of God as grower demonstrate that God's way of doing things in this world is *process.* Miracles, as the *extraordinary* speeding up of process, show that God is powerful enough to do whatever he wants however he wants. Growth, as the *ordinary* way things happen in the world, shows the way God has typically chosen to work in the world. If we insist that spiritual development occurs only in crisis events, we limit God and disregard his sovereign choice.

The apostle Paul recognized the vital process of planting, watering, and growing: "I planted the seed, Apollos watered it, but God made it grow. So neither he who plants nor he who waters is anything, but only God, who makes things grow" (1 Cor. 3:6–7). He spoke about growing in faith (2 Cor. 10:15), in love (Eph. 4:16), and in the knowledge of God (Col. 1:10). In Ephesians Paul uses an unusual expression: "Speaking the truth in love, we will in all things *grow up into him* who is the Head, that is, Christ" (4:15).

How does one "grow up into" someone? In Ephesians 4 Paul pictures the body growing together, "joined and held together by every supporting ligament" (v. 16). Without connective growth the body would contort and collapse into a pile of flesh and bone. But Christ holds it all together by growing it all together. Month by month, year by year, muscle, bone, tendon, and ligament are woven together in a process that began in "the secret place" of the womb (Ps. 139:15). Disease may intrude and disfigure; bodily trauma can disrupt the process; but through it all God irrepressibly grows "fearfully and wonderfully made" individuals (Ps. 139:14). What a marvel it is to see a human being go from hidden fetus to infant to child to adolescent to adult—almost two decades of bones growing longer, muscles stronger, senses trained, coordination tuned, voice richer. And we only see the gross movements of it all, the cellular and molecular knitting is left to the eyes of God alone. The same process happens spiritually as we "grow up into" Christ.

We should be awed by what God does in people during their first year or two of dramatic spiritual growth. They were spiritually empty, confused, and lost until they found God and opened their lives to his influence. As Peter says, they become "newborn babes" craving spiritual milk so that they can grow up in their salvation (1 Peter 2:2). They develop an appetite for spiritual truth and discover worship and service. In short, they grow in the grace and knowledge of Christ (2 Peter 3:18). It is the ultimate picture of divine work.

So how can spiritual leaders think of spiritual growth as anything but a marvel and a privilege? We're not biding our time waiting for people to grow, nor are we simply enduring the curse of this fallen world. The curse may interfere with growth, but growth itself is God's intentional work. We must believe that—even when we are frustrated by the spiritual childishness of some, or wild growth spurts of others that produce distorted theological ideas or misguided zeal. Phases of spiritual gangliness are part of "growing up."

The concept of growth influences our theology of ministry in many ways:

1. Spiritual life can only be a creation of God, for no mere mortal can claim credit for birth or growth.
2. We must not limit how God works to convert and sanctify people, but should be awed at his sovereign

power to produce growth. As Jesus said: "The Spirit gives birth to spirit. . . . The wind blows wherever it pleases. You hear its sound, but you cannot tell where it comes from or where it is going. So it is with everyone born of the Spirit" (John 3:6, 8).

3. Amazingly, God involves us in the process—be it planting, watering, or some other step.
4. Growth is development over time, and thus, cannot be forced.
5. Growth requires care and nourishment, and will be impeded in their absence.
6. Growth is not just increase, but shaping.
7. Just as the body's growth includes the knitting together of different kinds of tissues, spiritual growth involves the coordination of all of our inner faculties—our thinking, feeling, and willing.

We minister to people who "are being saved." Their growth is a life or death matter. We know they are growing when we see a fuller salvation, which is to say sin and Satan are less the victor, and the character of Christ becomes the contour of their lives.

Spiritual Development as Integration

When a body grows, its parts don't just get larger, they also become better connected. Nerves thicken and branch out, blood vessels and capillaries lengthen into every bit of living tissue, bones and joints are tied together by ligament and tendon. The result is an integrated physical organism. Every step that the body takes is an orchestration of energy, coordination, and will. Take these parts and train them, and a body is able to catch a football in full run, do a pirouette, or draw complex harmonies out of a piano.

There are so many parts to life—morals, aesthetics, relationships, ideas and opinions, social issues, health, the environment, community life, politics, marriage and family, church life. Without spiritual formation we move through life, bumping into these issues with randomness rather than with unity and wholeness. Spiritual development includes the progressive integration of *who we are,* of ourselves with the rest of *creation,* of our *relationships,* and of *aesthetics.*

Integrating Who We Are

A life of spiritual formation includes the intentional development and integration of a Christian mind, will, and affect. If these three are in principle held separate, or if one is developed and others are ignored, aberrations will result.

Favor the mind while devaluing the will and affect and you may end up a doctrine hound and a logic-chopper. Prefer will to the detriment of mind and affect and you develop a strong-arm, self-sufficient theology. Focus on affect while suppressing mind and will and you are at the mercy of your own subjectivism.

Every era has scholastics in tension with mystics, quietists being drowned out by activists, pietists trying to warm up the orthodox, militants burning the books of intellectuals. That will probably not change. The question is whether we believe in the value of the integrated self. "Love the Lord your God with all your heart, mind, soul, and strength" is the greatest of all commandments, and it surely includes every impulse, faculty, skill, and talent we possess.

Does this mean that the goal of ministry is to move toward a homogeneous ideal of a perfectly balanced Christian? Or can we find balance in the plurality of persons in the church? Surely the latter. Diversity in the church includes variations of psyche and temperament. Balance is in the body. Homogeneity within one person is not the goal because God has not chosen to make us that way. The work of spiritual growth is challenging enough without trying to move people to a uniform level of rationality, emotionality, and all the rest. There will always be those who read thick books and those who read thin ones, those who weep in worship and those who don't, those who drive like a bulldozer and those who are sensitized to every subtlety of life.

On the other hand, every person does possess the capacity for a life that is rational, emotional, and volitional. Exclude one and you have something not human. We cannot assign a part of our personhood to someone else in the body of Christ. The well-directed life is a harmony of the rational, emotional, and volitional that demonstrates the integrity (wholeness) of the person and the image of God mirrored in the person. And why does it all matter? It is not because these parts of ourselves all have a right to be heard, but because God had a purpose in mind when he gave us those faculties.

Many Christians can point to a time in their lives when spiritual growth awakened a part of themselves that had been asleep. Perhaps they had turned off their minds to be "spiritual" or they had discarded their emotions as a product of the flesh rather than the Creator. But one day they saw in someone they respected a Christ-centered, spiritually stable, genuinely full life. And they began to allow for themselves the formation of a previously unformed part of their lives. When a part of the self awakens to God, spiritual formation is occurring.

The word *heart,* as it appears in the Bible, refers to the core of our inner being in its fullness of mind, emotion, and will. It is the essence of personality, the seat of all motives. The very intent of the word is to point to integration. In the same way that the strength of a tree is found in a single trunk and its differentiation comes in the boughs, branches, and twigs, so spiritual growth in its parts is only as strong as the integration at its base.

We frequently minister to people who claim they are trying to "get their lives together." They are looking for concord at the core. Like the psalmists, pastors and other spiritual leaders must cheer people on to a bold unity of personhood that is found in the deepest place—the heart:

> You have filled my *heart* with greater joy
> than when their grain and new wine abound.
>
> Psalm 4:7

> I will praise you, O LORD, with all my *heart;*
> I will tell of all your wonders.
>
> Psalm 9:1

> The LORD is my strength and my shield;
> my *heart* trusts in him, and I am helped.
> My *heart* leaps for joy
> and I will give thanks to him in song.
>
> Psalm 28:7

> My *heart* is stirred by a noble theme
> as I recite my verses for the king;
> my tongue is the pen of a skillful writer.
>
> Psalm 45:1

> Create in me a pure *heart,* O God,
> and renew a steadfast spirit within me.
>
> Psalm 51:10

> Teach me your way, O LORD,
> and I will walk in your truth;

give me an undivided *heart,*
  that I may fear your name.
                      Psalm 86:11

I seek you with all my *heart;*
  do not let me stray from your commands.
I have hidden your word in my *heart*
  that I might not sin against you.
                      Psalm 119:10–11

I have chosen the way of truth;
  I have set my *heart* on your laws.
                      Psalm 119:30

Rulers persecute me without cause,
  but my *heart* trembles at your word.
                      Psalm 119:161

Search me, O God, and know my *heart;*
  test me and know my anxious thoughts.
                      Psalm 139:23

Let not my *heart* be drawn to what is evil,
  to take part in wicked deeds
with men who are evildoers;
  let me not eat of their delicacies.
                      Psalm 141:4

Isn't it interesting how often people will ask their teachers and preachers to speak to the heart? What they are asking for goes beyond sentimentality. If we think of heart as the core, the depth of the soul, then ministry that goes to the heart includes both the deepest thoughts and the deepest feelings. The "heartfelt religion" that the German Pietists of the seventeenth century (and others like them) promoted was not sentimental faith but deep faith.

Integrating Our Lives with the Rest of Creation

Spiritual development includes the progressive integration of all of who we are and also all of what life is. It's all there in the first two chapters of Genesis—first, the cosmos; then, man as the pinnacle of the creation; and finally, the relations of the inhabitants of the cosmos.

Spiritual vitality includes growing in understanding and awe of the creation of God. Out of the void God brought a natural, material universe of order, diversity, and unfathomable majesty. Light and darkness, dry land and sea, animals that fly, swim, or graze, deep blue and intense green, shrubs, flowers, fruit trees, and forests—they are all the sculptures of the one and only Creator.

> The heavens declare the glory of God;
> the skies proclaim the work of his hands.
> Day after day they pour forth speech;
> night after night they display knowledge.
> Psalm 19:1–2

Wise believers allow themselves to be awestruck by the glory of it all without crossing the line into adoration of the creation instead of the Creator. What a shame, however, when the noise of human activity or our own chauvinism causes us to give quick glances at the natural world, ignoring all the signs of his presence that God took time to place there.

Gnostics believe that the natural world has nothing to do with the realm of the spirit, but Christians should know better. Integrating the beauty, wonderment, and lessons of the natural world is an essential aspect of spiritual growth or formation. We are given sight, taste, touch, smell, and hearing—each an amazing gift of God—so that we may take in what God has created from "the beginning." We sometimes focus more on what our own hands have shaped out of concrete, plastic, polymers, or lumber—but if our horizons don't go beyond the city skyline and we don't know the world that God told Adam and Eve to care for, we know less of God and enjoy less of life.

Integrating Our Relationships

How many relationships do we have to figure out? Think about the labels: son, daughter, brother, sister, father, mother, husband, wife, student, teacher, employer, employee, friend, neighbor, aunt, uncle, grandfather, grandmother. What besides spiritual formation will spell the difference between a husband who is faithful or unfaithful, a loving or indifferent aunt, a good or a fair-weather friend? How can we possibly live up to our roles in any of these relationships without a spiritual understanding of it all?

When sin entered the world, relationships were immediately distorted. So the process of salvation includes the re-formation of relationships. Most dramatically, it includes the formation of love in the heart, a love which goes far beyond the limits of human instinct and self-interest. We learn to love what God loves. That's why Jesus' final conversation with Peter centered around the question, Do you love me? To love Jesus, as the Savior told Peter (and all shepherds), is to love what he loves. So he says, "Tend my sheep."

Integrating the Aesthetic Side of Life

Human life has an aesthetic pulse that should be synchronized with the rest of life. Music, for instance, can be as powerful as a tidal wave or as subtle and constant as a trickling stream. We shape it and it shapes us. Music surrounds us today and is so culturally influential that some people go so far as to submit their lives to the directives of their musical idols.

How amazing is the power of music to form us spiritually, and how frightening its potential to deform. That is why Martin Luther was taken with the powerful influence new forms of church music (congregational singing in the vernacular) could have during the Reformation, and why his Swiss contemporary, Ulrich Zwingli, retreated into minimalist psalm-singing without instrumentation. Both realized the spiritual power of music. Luther was willing to open the box, Zwingli held the lid tight.

Visual arts, graphic arts, photography, cinematography, and videography also shape us with their aesthetic appeal. Integrated into spiritual life, they offer to the ear, eye, smell, taste, and touch something that is suprarational, subjective by design. But aesthetics can also be the realm of lies and disconnected impulses, one more reason for the importance of spiritual formation.

Imagine, then, this kind of integrated, formed life— eyes open to the surrounding world, seeing God's greatness and mercy in it all; growing in love and in the practice of being a good friend, parent, leader, or citizen; accurately interpreting images on billboards, television, cinemas, and concert halls as well as the stream of information coming from the sciences; developing year by year in intellectual and emotional integrity; and making sound, willful decisions that reflect biblical values. The way to integrity (wholeness) is integration. It is when we behave the way we believe and our inner and outer lives become congruent. The alternative—contradiction instead of integration, hypocrisy instead of integrity—is the one thing for which Jesus reserved his severest condemnation.

Spiritual Development through Crisis

If you asked a wide variety of believers what was the most spiritually formative influence in their lives, what do you think they would say? Survey people and what you will find is that the most frequent answer is not "my mother," or "my home church," or "Pastor so-and-so." The most repeated influence is crisis.

Anybody who has been in ministry any length of time knows that crisis is an undeniable norm of life. There is "a time to weep and a time to laugh, a time to mourn and a time to dance" (Eccles. 3:4). The curse of Genesis 3 describes a world where pain, difficulty, enmity, and broken relationships are normal. Jesus said, "In this world you will have trouble" (John 16:33), and indeed a multitude of biblical stories—Joseph, Job, the Psalms, Lamentations—are stories of crisis and restoration. The wiser we are, the more we will expect the cracks and fissures of this life. As Ecclesiastes says: "For with much wisdom comes much sorrow; the more knowledge, the more grief" (1:18).

Crisis is one of the defining moments for grace. Life in this world produces "bruised reeds" and "smoldering wicks," and too often people's actions do not restore but rather they break the reed and snuff out the wick. Jesus does the opposite (Isa. 42:3). He demonstrates grace as he takes people who are on the brink and gives them a way to step back. The church must do the same. Whatever the crisis, the church has the opportunity to cushion the blow and to provide an environment where spiritual formation results. Without grace, crisis leaves people deformed, not formed.

The word *crisis* comes from the Greek and Latin words for decision or judgment, and indeed that is often the way crisis is experienced. It is a kind of judgment day, a day of decision. It reveals people for who they are, tearing down things that they thought were strong and important, and exposing the position of one's personality and faith. Crisis creates vacuum, providing an opportunity for God to fill the gap. Too often, though, people choose things such as relationships, entertainment, or alcohol to fill the void. That's why crisis is the preeminent moment for the church to show itself at its best—as a community that offers a lifeline. People who have been caught in the loving arms of this community will never forget it, and it will inevitably become one of the truly formative experiences of their lives.

> Who but you, Lord, could bring sweetness in the midst of bitterness, pleasure in the midst of torment? How wonderful are the wounds in my soul, since the deeper the wound, the greater is the joy of healing!
>
> John of the Cross (1542–1591)

Crisis as Forced Formation

We have been talking in this book about change in the sense of formation or transformation. Normally we think of this as an active process, but crisis is really a kind of forced change. When a young mother dies from cancer, small children, a bewildered husband, extended family, friends, and church acquaintances are forced to see that we live in a broken, fallen, and diseased world. The word *change* seems a gross understatement for this kind of dramatic, life-altering event. Just as the moon's path would be radically altered if the earth disappeared, we may also be set on an erratic path when a loved one is ripped from our lives.

Depending on the circumstances, crisis may force changed assumptions about safety, health, relationships, social station, what we really value in life, and our futures. It pushes peripheral things to the margins of life and focuses our attention on things that matter. Suddenly houses and boats and bank accounts seem trivial, and things such as family and relationships with others take center stage. People plunged into crisis often wonder why they have been investing so much of their time and energy in things that now seem not at all important. Crisis strips us down to the soul; it forms us by reducing us.

While we may speak about crisis as an opportunity for spiritual growth, we should avoid any glibness about it. To dismiss people's pain or give facile answers is to violate the church's call to be an instrument of mercy. And mercy is very often all that people in crisis have to go on. Weak and weary, it may be all they can do to call out to God for mercy. And that is exactly the request we should make on their behalf. Crisis shows that we are indeed "frail children of dust, and feeble as frail." As the apostle Paul puts it:

> We have this treasure in jars of clay to show that this all-surpassing power is from God and not from us. We are hard pressed on every side, but not crushed; perplexed, but not in despair; persecuted, but not abandoned; struck down, but not destroyed. We always carry around in our body the death of Jesus, so that the life of Jesus may also be revealed in our body.
>
> 2 Corinthians 4:7–10

The mercy of God is what allows people to be survivors instead of victims. Survivors draw on their resources to persist through difficult circumstances.

The Christian Community as a Haven for Healing

The church is to be a haven for healing. People who have gone through crisis need a refuge, a sanctuary, a safe place—a community that does not dissect, evaluate, or manipulate their souls, but rather allows them to reside with others under God's restorative power. The church, as "the house of mourning," provides safe, familiar surroundings with people bound by the covenant of God and committed to the longsuffering ministry of presence. They minister and heal by just "being there." We must trust that healing takes place even in hidden places too complex and microscopic for our eyes to detect. God makes it happen or it doesn't happen at all.

Progress of spiritual formation following crisis may be so gradual that it cannot be detected on a week-by-week basis. Or there may be spurts of spiritual strengthening followed by setbacks. The challenge for observers is to stay out of the way of God's healing power, providing words and deeds of comfort in the form of grace and truth, but resisting the idea that we can rebuild somebody's life from the inside out.

Hope for restoration, but know that remaining scars do not signal spiritual defeat. The marks in Jesus' hands and feet did not nullify the power of his resurrection. Sooner or later we will all face crisis and have the opportunity to join with the community of the cured.

So how can Christian leaders build and maintain a community conducive for healing? Here are some practical suggestions for teaching and ministry in the midst of crises:

Teach about the mysterious, restorative work of God in the hidden places of the heart.

Build familiarity with the many stories of injury and healing in the biblical narrative.

Challenge people to faith in the restorative power of God.

Encourage people to simply be present for people in crisis.

Warn people against simplistic, crude expectations for people who are going through crisis.

Define spiritual progress as nothing more and nothing less than what the biblical text says it is.

Assure people that God's grace is sometimes found in simple survival, and that strengthening will happen with the passage of time.

Challenge people to set aside their own selfish desires that people in crisis stop being needy.

Teach people that emotional swings are part of grief and trauma, and that hurting people need a listening ear and encouragement to bring their pain and questions to God.

Promote readiness in prayer. Have groups of people who are ready and willing to receive crisis prayer requests and who will be faithful in following through in prayer. Much is gained with the understanding that the first thing the church will do for someone in crisis is to pray.

Develop support groups in the church or in the community that put people in contact with others who have faced similar crises (e.g. loss of a child, loss of a spouse, alcohol or drug abuse). Contrary to some people's fears and suspicions, support groups do not perpetuate problems if they are well-led. And the church is a natural context for such support.

Develop in all areas of ministry a network of small groups, and promote caring as one of the basic purposes of each group. A group will react instinctively to support someone they already know.

Be familiar with available mental health resources for cases where crisis results in mental or emotional disorders.

As mysterious and as wonderful as spiritual birth is, spiritual growth is no less so. Growing means increase—of knowledge, of experience, and of maturity—but it also means formation. It is a process of *integrating* all aspects of life, and even when *crisis* breaks us down, God's grace is there to put the pieces back together in brand new forms. And God puts the church there as the instrument of soul-shaping.

War against the Soul

Sin as Deformation

Almighty and most merciful Father; We have erred, and strayed from thy ways like lost sheep. We have followed too much the devices and desires of our own hearts. We have offended against thy holy laws. We have left undone those things which we ought to have done; And we have done those things which we ought not to have done; And there is no health in us. But thou, O Lord, have mercy upon us, miserable offenders. Spare thou those, O God, who confess their faults. Restore thou those who are penitent; According to thy promises declared unto mankind in Jesus Christ our Lord. And grant, O most merciful Father, for his sake; That we may hereafter live a godly, righteous, and sober life, To the glory of thy Holy Name. Amen.

A General Confession
Book of Common Prayer

For ten years Susan reveled in the new life she found in God and in the church. Her life was now full of Bible studies, choir practices, and youth groups—completely different from the bar life and hidden bottles that had been her obsession. She remarried, finished her degree, and even began a new ministry for unwed mothers. She pursued physical fitness until she had a magazine-cover physique. Yet she was never happy, always restless. Lost and empty inside, she moved from one desperate obsession to the next. It shocked everyone when she expressed hints of doubt about her faith, then dropped out of the church entirely and expressed cynicism about it all. She left her husband, embittered her children, and seemed to drop off the edge of the earth. Susan had gone through the motions for ten years, so she left behind family and friends bewildered about what had happened. Her life demonstrated the tragic side of the parable of the sower—soil that is too shallow or too rocky or too thorny cannot really accept the seed.

Another Law at Work

In 1 Peter 2 we find an ominous description of the aggressive attacks of sin: "Dear friends, I urge you, as aliens and strangers in the world, to abstain from sinful desires, which war against your soul" (v. 11). The struggle against sin does indeed seem like a war of the worst kind—a civil war. There are external evil enemies, to be sure, but the real battleground is right within the soul, and it is often the self which is the self's own worst enemy.

Ministry that goes no further than the externals is no ministry at all. We should know that, but sometimes it takes years of ministry to be heartbroken enough by the sight of human wreckage to realize that the formation of persons in the inmost parts is not a superficial business. The church is not a first aid station where Band-Aids and aspirin are blithely distributed. It's a trauma center where broken and bleeding persons arrive daily, many of them unaware of just how injured they are. The attending physician is God the Holy Spirit whose work it is to take what is deformed and to form it into the image of God.

People must be spiritually formed both because any growing thing must have pattern and organization to its growth, and because there is a power at work in us that persistently *de*forms and *dis*figures. As Paul puts it in Romans 7:

> So I find this law at work: When I want to do good, evil is right there with me. For in my inner being I delight in God's law; but I see another law at work in the members of my body, waging war against the law of my mind and making me a prisoner of the law of sin at work within my members.
>
> verses 21–23

Sin is a law at work in the sense that it is universal, persistent, and chronic. Honest spiritual leaders don't deny it in themselves, and they don't sugarcoat it in their congregations. John Chrysostom, Archbishop of Constantinople at the beginning of the fifth century and one of the greatest preachers of all time, said of his long-standing efforts as a pastor: "My work is like that of a man who is trying to clean a piece of ground into which a muddy stream is constantly flowing." Yet Chrysostom was not sour on his role. He also said: "My congregation is my crown of glory, and every single listener means more to me than all the rest of the city."

The Vocabulary of Sin

Helping people in spiritual formation includes helping them understand the deforming effects of sin. If we speak biblically, we will find that there is almost no topic where God's glory *and* the brokenness of humanity do not surface.

Consider the range of the biblical vocabulary of sin which includes the notion of conscious rebellion:

Term	Meaning	References	Manifestation
chata' (Heb.)	to miss a mark or a way; to sin	Exodus 10:16	we fall short
pasha' (Heb.)	to rebel, transgress, or revolt	2 Kings 8:20 Psalm 5:10 Ezekiel 2:3	we purposely disobey God's law
awah (Heb.)	to distort, to make crooked, to pervert (includes sin and its consequences)	Job 33:27 Psalm 106:43 Isaiah 30:13	in thought, word, and deed we show the twisting of our souls
shagah (Heb.)	to go astray, stray, err	Proverbs 19:27 Isaiah 28:7 Ezekiel 34:6	we make mistakes
hamartia (Gk.)	sin, to miss	Matthew 9:13	we miss the mark
adikia (Gk.)	injustice, wrong, injury	Romans 2:8 1 John 5:17	we violate standards of justice
parabasis (Gk.)	transgression	Romans 2:23; 4:15 James 2:9	we deviate from God's direction
paraptōma (Gk.)	transgression, trespass, sin	Romans 5:15-20; 11:11-12	we deliberately fall to the side of God's way
anomia (Gk.)	lawlessness, being without law	1 Corinthians 9:21 2 Corinthians 6:14 Hebrews 1:9 1 John 3:4	we show ignorance or indifference toward God's law

It would be simpler for us if "sin" only meant conscious, deliberate acts of rebellion, but the biblical vocabulary includes falling short, living out distortions of the psyche, and even unwitting mistakes. Yet it doesn't stop there. The face of sin is also described as blindness or darkness, selfishness, godlessness, evil.

This, then, is what we are up against. The goal of Christian ministry is to help people be spiritually shaped, but the opposing forces at work are as unintentional as wandering and as blatant as rebellion. In sin we injure and are injured. We victimize and are victims. Fallenness includes rebellion and mistakes, obsessions, compulsions and addictions, and the environments and heritage which prompt them. If our theology embraces the whole range of fallen behavior described in the Scriptures, then we have no alternative but to see cracks and fissures running through who we are and what our world is. Sin is not an occasional crisis; it is the way things are. It makes the whole creation groan (Rom. 8:22).

Being Bent

How would you explain sin to someone who had never seen it? In *Perelandra,* C. S. Lewis's protagonist has to do just that for a race of beings who have known only Paradise. The protagonist says wicked men are "bent ones," an allusion to the biblical description of human beings as crooked people with crooked ways, twisted and malformed, looking majestic at times but then distorted in sometimes comical, sometimes tragic ways. We are crooked.

This is also a reminder of the classical Christian belief that sin is not an alien power or an infecting germ. It would be easier to deal with if it were an external contaminant, but the fact of the matter is that sin is the way we are. It is the twisted shape of something created good. Gluttony is exaggerated consumption, theft is unregulated desire, lust is misdirected passion, pride (in the bad sense) is pride (in the good sense) that has gone up one too many rungs on the ladder or has an attitude of one-upmanship. Even Satan is a good angel who is twisted. To produce darkness, all you need do is remove light.

Depravity is not the belief that we are beyond hope or that we are as bad as we can be, but rather it is the belief that we are crooked in every faculty we possess.

I've often found a simple illustration helpful on this point. Take a piece of clean white paper and, with a pencil, smear it with lines and smudges. This is the way we typically think of sin, as a substance that has stained and sullied the purity of the white paper. Now take another clean sheet of paper, crumple it into a ball, and then straighten it out. Now the imperfections in the paper are not due to the presence of an external element. The wrinkles and creases are part of the condition of the paper itself. One can make improvements by straightening the paper and trying to press out the wrinkles, but the creases will not disappear. The same is true of sin. It is not a foreign infection, something imposed on us; it is our very condition, a condition which has affected every faculty. Only a dramatic divine work of spiritual formation will help bent people become straight again.

This is the arena for ministry—crooked people living crooked lives in a crooked world. No wonder the apostle Paul, writing to his dear friends in Philippi, pleaded for their obedience though they lived in a "crooked" generation:

> Therefore, my dear friends, as you have always obeyed . . . continue to work out your salvation with fear and trembling, for it is God who works in you to will and to act according to his good purpose. . . . so that you may become blameless and pure, children of God without fault in a crooked and depraved generation, in which you shine like stars in the universe as you hold out the word of life—in order that I may boast on the day of Christ that I did not run or labor for nothing.
>
> Philippians 2:12–13, 15–16

Paul believed that people really are disfigured, but that they, by the power of God, can shine like the stars! To the Corinthians Paul said,

> Neither the sexually immoral nor idolaters nor adulterers nor male prostitutes nor homosexual offenders nor thieves nor the greedy nor drunkards nor slanderers nor swindlers will inherit the kingdom of God. And that is what some of you were. But you were washed, you were sanctified, you were justified in the name of the Lord Jesus Christ and by the Spirit of our God.
>
> 1 Corinthians 6:9–11

Only Christian ministry purports to take on such an impossible situation. Easier religions soften the crisis and tone down the cure, but in Christianity we accept a view of a mangled humanity being untwisted and reformed by the gracious hand of God.

Two Prescriptions

Two great pastors give advice on the subject of how to deal with transgression in the heart. We must understand their words in the context of their time and culture, but because human nature is basically the same today as it was then, their counsel endures.

John Wesley's Analysis of Sin in the Life of the Believer

Some have tried to help Christians deal with sin through understanding its etiology. That's what James does in James 1:13–15. John Wesley gives this analysis:

1. The divine seed of loving, conquering faith, remains in him that is born of God. "He keepeth himself" by the grace of God and "cannot commit sin."
2. A temptation arises; whether from the world, the flesh, or the devil, it matters not.
3. The Spirit of God gives him warning that sin is near, and bids him more abundantly watch unto prayer.
4. He gives way, in some degree, to the temptation, which now begins to grow pleasing to him.
5. The Holy Spirit is grieved; his faith is weakened; and his love of God grows cold.
6. The Spirit reproves him more sharply and saith, "This is the way, walk thou in it."
7. He turns away from the painful voice of God and listens to the pleasing voice of the tempter.
8. Evil desire begins and spreads in his soul, till faith and love vanish away; he is then capable of committing outward sin, the power of the Lord being departed from him.[1]

Wesley wants to help believers understand the subtle inner voices that are part of the process of sin. This chorus of voices include the world, the flesh, the devil, the Spirit of God, and the human soul that is a mixture of faith, love, and evil desire. Wesley's analysis emphasizes the complexity of our actions and is a reminder to shepherds that spiritual formation includes educating people as to what motivates them so they can anticipate the spiritual crossroads they will face every day.

John Owen's "The Preparation for Mortification"

At the end of one of his treatises on sin, John Owen, the seventeenth-century Puritan theologian, lays out a plan for the mortification of sinful attitudes and deeds in the life of the believer.

1. Consider whether the sin exhibits particularly dangerous symptoms.
2. Maintain a clear and abiding sense of guilt, danger, and evil of sin.
3. Let the guilty weight of sin burden your conscience.
4. Seek with a constant longing to be delivered from the power of sin.
5. Consider if the evil perplexing you is rooted in your nature, and nurtured and exaggerated by your temperament.
6. Watch out for the occasions when your evil sickness tends to occur.
7. React strongly against the first stirrings of your evil disposition.
8. Use meditation as a means of self-abasement by contemplating God's perfection and your sinfulness.
9. Take care that you do not speak peace to yourself before God speaks it.

Owen's emphasis is sober awareness. Be aware of sin's power, its subtlety, and the situations which might make you more vulnerable to temptation. One might say that dependence on the Spirit should be brought out more prominently in this list, but Owen assumes the Christian will know to do that. The awareness Owen calls us to is important because sin is beguiling. It hides behind denial and rationalizations.

Biblical teaching about sin leaves us with a life or death scenario. Sin will kill spiritual life, but spiritual birth and development hold the prospect of transformation itself.

From Text to Godliness

Formative Reading

> May your Spirit, O Christ, lead me in the right
> way, keeping me safe from all forces of evil and
> destruction. And, free from all malice, may I search
> diligently in your Holy Word to discover with the
> eyes of my mind your commandments. Finally, give
> me the strength of will to put those command-
> ments into practice through all the days of my life.
>
> Bede (c. 673–735)

Take Up and Read

The defining moment in what many have called the
greatest autobiography of all time takes place when a
man's eyes fall on a text. Augustine of Hippo, a rebel
against Christianity, was filled with its teaching and cap-
tivated by its appeal, but had not allowed himself to
believe. He needed just one tap and he would fall into
the faith that lay before him like a whole new world.

One day Augustine heard a voice as of a child playing some kind of game say what sounded like, *"Tole lege, tole lege"* (Take up and read, take up and read). Augustine tells us what happened next:

> I snatched [a copy of the epistles] up, opened it, and read in silence the chapter on which my eyes first fell: "Not in rioting and drunkenness, not in chambering and impurities, not in strife and envying; but you put on the Lord Jesus Christ, and make not provision for the flesh . . ." No further wished I to read, nor was there need to do so. Instantly, in truth, at the end of this sentence, as if before me a peaceful light streaming into my heart, all the dark shadows of doubt fled away.[1]

Although this is not the typical experience of daily Scripture reading, it may be what God chooses to do here and there when he knows we need a crisis experience to arrest our attention and shatter our presumptions or idolatry. Regardless, Scripture reading should be a block-by-block building of ideas, images, exhortations, and oracles into a complete, structured vision of reality.

The Importance of Reading

Some of the brightest leaders in the Christian church have pleaded with its shepherds to stay committed in their own spiritual growth through reading:

> Watch, study, give attendance to reading! Verily, you cannot read too well; and what you read well you cannot understand too well; and what you understand well you cannot teach too well;

and what you teach well you cannot live too well! *Experto crede ruperto* (believe one who knows by experience). It is the devil, it is the world, it is our flesh, that rage and rave against us. Therefore, dear sirs and brethren, pastors and preachers, pray, read, study, be diligent! Verily, there is no time for sloth, snoring, and sleeping in this evil, shameful time. Use the gift that has been committed to you and make known the mystery of Christ. If a man does not want to know, let him be ignorant, as Paul says in I Corinthians 14:38. We must not fail to proclaim the Word of mystery simply because we have baptism and the Sacrament. Things will be well when we have done our part.

Martin Luther[2]

Do you then, my son, diligently apply yourself to the reading of the sacred Scriptures. Apply yourself, I say. For we who read the things of God need much application, lest we should say or think anything too rashly about them. And applying yourself thus to the study of the things of God, with faithful prejudgments such as are well pleasing to God, knock at its locked door, and it will be opened to you by the porter of whom Jesus says, "To him the porter opens." Any applying yourself thus to the divine study, seek aright, and with unwavering trust in God, the meaning of the Holy Scriptures, which so many have missed. Be not satisfied with knocking and seeking; for prayer is of all things indispensable to the knowledge of the things of God. For to this the Saviour exhorted, and said not only, "Knock, and it shall be opened to you; and seek, and ye shall find," but also, "Ask, and it shall be given unto you."

Origen[3]

Study hard, for the well is deep, and our brains are shallow. But especially be laborious in practice and in the exercise of your knowledge.

Richard Baxter[4]

Apply thyself wholly to the text; apply the matter wholly to thyself.

Johann Albrecht Bengel[5]

It is not many books or much reading that makes men learned; but it is good things, however little of them, often read, that make men learned in the Scriptures and make them godly, too. Indeed the writings of all the holy fathers should be read only for a time, in order that through them we may be led to the Holy Scriptures. We are like men who study the signposts and never travel the road. The dear fathers wished, by their writings, to lead us to the Scriptures, though the Scriptures alone are our vineyard in which we all ought to work and toil.

Martin Luther[6]

The voices of the past call out again and again, pleading with us to be filled with the grace and truth of God that is available through the written word.

Reading is not the specialized interest of heady Christians. Bookishness is not the mark of orthodoxy nor its invalidation. Material read most certainly varies from one believer to another and from one leader to another, but whether or not to read is not the issue. The reason is rooted in the very way God revealed himself.

Christianity is a religion of the Book. Jesus is the Word behind the words. Visions, oracles, histories, poetry—it's all there in black and white. It began when God's finger traced the very letters of the Decalogue on tablets of stone and inaugurated the process of truth in writing. But a golden calf and revelry were more interesting than tablets of stone to God's first audience, and ever since we have had a hard time settling down to let God speak to us through his written word. So how can we encourage people to read in a culture clearly more enamored with cellulose film and CRT screens than with ink on paper?

Encouraging People to Read

They say you can lead a horse to water, but you can't make him drink. Perhaps the same can be said of reading for spiritual growth. There are innumerable ways in which we can lead people to real words of life, but doing the reading will always be up to them. There are some things, however, that will encourage them down that road.

Model Reading

We must model an attitude of reverence for and excitement about Scripture, and we must show people how to read it systematically and thoughtfully.

When a pastor quotes books and articles he has read, at least a few people will jot down a title or make a mental note to look for it. The majority of the people may not do so, but that doesn't mean that the preacher shouldn't have bothered. There will always be at least a subset of people who read the Bible faithfully and thoughtfully, subscribe to substantive Christian journals, or even read the church newsletter thoroughly. Sometimes we make the mistake of thinking that we must figure out what the congregation is reading, read that ourselves, and quote from it to make a credible point with the congregation. Grocery store magazines become the authentication of the message. But this method turns things around. It may be true that a pastor will benefit by knowing what the people are reading, but the opportunity exists to lead them on to deeper reading by alluding to, quoting, and reviewing things that are on the horizon of their reading. People are encouraged when they sense that their leaders are teaching them out of a full well of water—that each bucket is filled for the present time and will be refilled upon the people's return.

There is a danger here. Teachers and pastors must not use quotations and allusions to validate themselves before the congregation. When the motive is to impress people, you risk separation from them. Clerical elitism does not encourage people to read; or if it does, it tempts them to find impressive snippets rather than rivers of truth. Spiritual formation through reading (or for that matter, through prayer, fellowship, service, or any other form) is for the purpose of making people Christlike, not Phariseelike.

Books of quotes will never equal a mind well-packed with the treasures found through good reading. So John Wesley urged a fellow pastor:

> What has exceedingly hurt you in time past, nay, and I fear, to this day, is, want of reading. I scarce ever knew a preacher read so little. And perhaps, by neglecting it, have lost the taste for it. Hence your talent in preaching does not increase. It is just the same as it was seven years ago. It is lively, but not deep; there is little variety; there is no compass of thought. Reading only can supply this, with meditation and daily prayer. . . . O begin! Fix some part of every day for private exercise. You may acquire the taste which you have not: what is tedious at first, will afterward be pleasant. Whether you like it or no, read and pray

daily. It is for your life; there is no other way; else you will be a trifler all your days, and a pretty, superficial preacher. Do justice to your own soul; give it time and means to grow. Do not starve yourself any longer. Take up your cross and be a Christian altogether. Then will all the children of God rejoice (not grieve) over you.[7]

These are strong words. Yet if any of us sat under the preaching of John Wesley, we would undoubtedly know how deep was the well from which he drew.

Prescribe Reading

Churches that set aside space for libraries or for the sale of periodicals and books take a proactive approach in leading people into spiritual reading. The church newsletter can be a great place for recommended reading lists or reprinting (with permission) quality articles. Congregations are deeply grateful when their leaders show them devotional materials that can help them with daily Bible reading and prayer. A church may even elect to publish its own material periodically.

People pay attention when their leaders say, "This book changed my life," or when someone lists the most helpful books for different life circumstances (e.g., mourning, child-rearing, evangelism, etc.). Christian magazines often publish lists of the year's best books—pass them along to the congregation.

How We Read

We have all read things that have had no formative influence on us. Perhaps what we chose to read had nothing that would shape us, or maybe we did not comprehend it or we prevented ourselves from being influenced. Just as a spouse can nod and say, "uh-huh," claiming all the time to be listening, we can read in such a way that the words go through our brains but don't find their way into our hearts.

In his book, *Shaped by the Word,* Robert Mulholland draws a distinction between formational reading and informational reading.

> We tend to think of informational and formational reading as two different techniques for reading. The real issue is not a matter of which technique is best or even what is the optimum combination of techniques, but rather what posture toward the mystery of God can open us up to formational possibilities.[8]

Reading so that we are shaped is not a matter of posture, place, time, or other technique. These are minor influences, whereas the real issue is one of heart attitude. Mulholland describes formational reading in these ways:

Formational reading is not concerned with quantity.

Informational reading is linear; formational reading is in-depth.

Informational reading's task is to master the text; formational reading's purpose is for the text to master you.

With formational reading, "instead of the text being an object we control . . . the text becomes the subject of the reading relationship; we are the object that is shaped by the text."

"Instead of the analytical, critical, judgmental approach of informational reading, formational reading requires a humble, detached, willing, loving approach."

Informational reading is problem solving; formational reading is openness to mystery.[9]

Richard Foster speaks about the time-honored *lectio divina* (divine reading):

> This is a kind of reading in which the mind descends into the heart, and both are drawn into the love and goodness of God. We are doing more than reading words; we are seeking "the Word exposed in the words," to use the phrase of Karl Barth. We are endeavoring to go beyond information to formation—to being formed and molded by what we read. We are listening with the heart to the Holy within. This prayerful reading, as we might call it, transforms us and strengthens us.[10]

There are then, these three elements: reading, meditation, and prayer. For many people meditation may come the hardest. We can discipline ourselves to spend time reading, and we know what it is to pray after we read, but it can be so difficult to take even a few minutes to stop and think about what we have read.

Got the reading *done!* That is often what we think when we slap shut the pages. Even if we are reading entirely on our own, not by someone else's assignment, reading sometimes is nothing more than one more check off the list. In our minds it is one more spiritual accomplishment, one more point toward some invisible merit badge. We trust that somehow, sometime, what we have read will connect with our souls. But for now, it's time to go on to other things. After all, we wouldn't want someone to think that we were lazy! The truth is, however, that one of the most important things we can do to be shaped by the good words we read is to allow time for reflection. During such time is when the mind does its amazing work of synthesizing new information with the multitude of ideas already stored, and it's when the Holy Spirit makes connections between new insights and old issues in our lives.

What We Read

Reading of Scripture, of course, is primary. In *Notes on the Old Testament* John Wesley gave specific advice on how to read Scripture devoutly, regularly, and effectively:

> If you desire to read the Scriptures in such a manner as may most effectually answer this end, would it not be advisable, (1) To set apart a little time, if you can, every morning and evening for that purpose? (2) At each time, if you have leisure, to read a chapter out of the Old and one out of the New Testament; if you cannot do this, to take a single chapter, or a part of one? (3) To read this with a single eye, to know the whole will of God, and a fixed resolution to do it? In order to know His will, you should, (4) Have a constant eye to the analogy of faith, the connexion and harmony there is between those grand, fundamental doctrines, original sin, justification by faith, the new birth, inward and outward holiness: (5) Serious and earnest prayer should be constantly used before we consult the oracles of God; seeing 'Scripture can only be understood through the same Spirit whereby it was given.' Our reading should likewise be closed with prayer, that what we read may be written on our hearts: (6) It might also be of use, if, while we read, we were frequently to pause, and examine ourselves by what we read, both with regard to our hearts and lives. . . . And whatever light you then receive should be used to the uttermost, and that immediately. Let there

be no delay. Whatever you resolve begin to execute the first moment you can. So shall you find this word to be indeed the power of God unto present and eternal salvation.[11]

Then, there are the Christian classics that have stood the test of time. We would all do well to heed C. S. Lewis's advice when he said that we should not neglect the reading of old books out of a sense that the newest is always the best. There is no good reason for us to peer down our noses at writers of the past because we know better today. Yes, it can be a stretch to get used to the language of past cultures, but it may not be as hard as we think, and we do it all the time when we read the Bible. We look very Darwinized when we perpetuate the modern assumption that the latest (i.e., the last step in evolution) is always the best. The latest, greatest book may have the nicest looking cover and typescript, but it may be out of print in two years. In contrast, a wealth of older books have been in demand for decades or even centuries.

There is only so much time we have to read, so it is important to be selective. We should read what has stood the test of time, we should read new books that come recommended by reliable people, and we should read what will stretch us.

Dialogue with God

Formative Prayer

Lord, teach us to pray. Some of us are not skilled in the art of prayer. As we draw near to thee in thought, our spirits long for thy Spirit, and reach out for thee, longing to feel thee near. We know not how to express the deepest emotions that lie hidden in our hearts.

In these moments, we have no polished phrases with which to impress one another, no finely moulded, delicately turned clauses to present to thee. Nor would we be confined to conventional petitions and repeat our prayers like the unwinding of a much-exposed film. We know, our Father that we are praying most when we are saying least. We know that we are closest to thee when we have left behind the things that have held us captive so long.

We would not be ignorant in prayer and, like children, make want lists for thee. Rather, we pray that thou wilt give unto us only what we really need. We would not make our prayers the importuning of thee, an omnipotent God, to do what we want thee to do. Rather, give us the vision, the courage, that shall enlarge our horizons and stretch our faith to the adventure of seeking thy loving will for our lives.

We thank thee that thou art hearing us even now. We thank thee for the grace of prayer. We thank thee for thyself.

Peter Marshall (1902–1949)

The Incense of the Church

The last scriptural teaching about prayer is an image and a scent. From bowls made of gleaming gold and filled with smoldering incense, wisps of smoke waft upward, pungent to anyone standing nearby, but especially so to the God to whom they are directed. These are "the prayers of all the saints" (Rev. 5:8; 8:3–4). We are supposed to associate this with the smoke of Old Testament sacrifices—"an offering made by fire, a pleasing aroma" to God. Now prayer and praise is at the center of our sacrifice to God. "Through Jesus, therefore, let us continually offer to God a sacrifice of praise—the fruit of lips that confess his name" (Heb. 13:15).

Perhaps we could be inspired by imagining an angel assigned to our churches, an angel like the one in Revelation who holds a golden bowl of incense that is the prayers of the saints in our churches. A pleasing aroma goes forth to God from our prayer meetings, Bible studies, worship services, hospital rooms, youth groups—wherever sincere prayers are offered to God. There are also multitudes of private prayers offered by people in their kitchens, their cars, their offices, their bedrooms. These are the hidden prayers, the "secret" prayers that

Jesus promoted (Matt. 6:6). Taken all together these prayers are short and long, spontaneous and planned, composed and extemporaneous, shouted and whispered. God takes them all.

That we should pray is a given. We will also assume that most of us long for more prayer in our lives and in the lives of our congregations. But before we talk about promoting prayer in the local congregation, let us consider what it is about prayer that is spiritually formative. It's easy to set up prayer programs, push people to participate, then complain when they don't and begin the cycle again. In doing so we miss the point, though. Prayer is not to be done for prayer's sake, and prayer vitality is not measured simply by the number of prayer programs we promote. Prayer is about God and our link with God. Prayer is a dialogue. It is speaking and listening, always believing that the voice of God will be louder than our own.

It is perfectly appropriate to speak about the subjective influence of prayer. Some theologies promote the idea that prayer does something to God; others stress that it does something to the world. Our focus in this chapter is what prayer does to us. As we will see, the biblical authors had much to say about the influence of prayer on spiritual development.

All of us desire to be faithful in prayer, to have it flow through our lives and be as natural as anything else. We frequently wrestle with prayer because a multitude of other things crowd it out, and it takes faith and patience to believe that prayer is worth our time. But as John Stott points out, prayer in its best form is a direct extension of our created humanity:

> Men and women are at their noblest and best
> when they are on their knees before God in prayer.
> To pray is not only to be truly godly; it is also to be

truly human. For here are human beings, made by God like God and for God, spending time in fellowship with God. So prayer is an authentic activity in itself, irrespective of any benefits it may bring us. Yet it is also one of the most effective of all means of grace. I doubt if anybody has ever become at all Christlike who has not been diligent in prayer. "What is the reason," asked Bishop J. C. Ryle, "that some believers are so much brighter and holier than others?" "I believe the difference," he answered himself, "in nineteen cases out of twenty, arises from different habits about private prayer. I believe that those who are not eminently holy pray *little* and those who are eminently holy pray *much*." Again, "prayer and sinning will never live together in the same heart. Prayer will consume sin, or sin will choke prayer."[1]

Prayer as Spiritual Awareness

When we speak to God a certain awareness of our relationship with him is pressed upon the soul—and thereby the soul is shaped. It begins to happen the moment prayer begins. It is rooted in the profound fact that we are actually speaking and listening to Almighty God. Slowly, incrementally, with each passing day, with each sincere prayer, our souls rehearse certain truths about our relationship with God, not because the truths are verbalized but because they are enacted. Through progressive soul-shaping dialogue with God we gain a spiritual consciousness that we are *under* God, *with* God, *in* God, and *for* God.

Prayer as Position: "We Are under God"

Every prayer reinforces the truth that we are under God. We need to teach people that we pray in order to position ourselves properly in the world and before God. We are under God. That is why we sometimes bow in prayer, or lift faces and hands toward God in receptivity, or lie down in complete submission (the repeated image of the twenty-four elders of Revelation). This is why we are conscious of our posture when we pray. We have an instinct that tells us that when we pray we are positioning ourselves before God with deliberate consciousness of who he is and who we are in relation to him.

Prayer can and should humble a worship team about to go out and lead a congregation in worship. The musicians, the preacher, the readers, the audio technician come with natural distractions and peculiar priorities, but in a moment of quiet, reverent, genuine prayer, they realize that they are under the majesty and grace of the Lord of the universe. A few minutes of prayer has the power to shape their disposition for that all-important hour and in turn to shape the worship experience of the whole congregation.

In a small group there may be friction or out-and-out animosity between members. Others may not be sure of their standing in the group. But in a time of prayer the heart of each person can be humbled and raised by the very posture of prayer.

People who are leveled by suffering often throw themselves down in prayer, if not physically, at least in attitude. Consider Jesus who fell face down in Gethsemane. People who pray for suffering individuals can minister by simply submitting to the mercies of God. People prayed for in this way often feel uplifted in that moment and for that day. Consequently, they are able to dry their tears and take the next steps that lie before them.

A preacher preparing the Sunday message must speak from the looming authority of the Word. Prayer can produce the appropriate emotional and mental posture for preaching. It begins with prayers for the preparation of the message during the week and continues when the preacher prays with quietness and brevity just before stepping up to speak.

We could extend these examples to every venue of life. Prayer is position.

Prayer as Presence: "We Are with God"

Prayer shapes our conviction that God is "with us." The moment we begin to pray (unless we believe we are speaking to the open air), we are impressed with the truth that there is a God who is within earshot, cares to listen, and has invited us to speak. We are with God and he is with us. That is one of the truths that God speaks most frequently. It appears on practically every page in the Bible. It is the reality of the garden in Genesis and the new Jerusalem in Revelation. It is the great truth God broadcast to the patriarchs, to the exodus generation, to the exiles in Babylon, and to the nation's rebuilders. It is the truth of Jesus' words in the upper room and at his ascension.

When we pray, we confess this truth and we bolster it in our minds.

Prayer as Power: "We Are in God"

What do we believe about our proximity to God when we pray? Sometimes prayers are cast out as across a vast distance. One person described this phenomenon, saying, "We think here that the Almighty is hard of hearing." Sometimes we pray as if God is right next to us. And sometimes our prayers show a spiritual awareness that we are in God and God, in the person of his Spirit, is in us. If we are in God prayer does not need to be sent to God; the act of prayer is direct communion with God. Belief in divine transcendence ensures that we will not confuse ourselves with God, and belief in divine immanence assures us that there is no chasm prayer needs cross except the gaps made within us by our sin.

If, in prayer, we grow in our consciousness that we are in God (i.e., in Christ, in the Spirit), then we grow also in the awareness that the power of God is at hand in any circumstance, for any reason. "Power in prayer" is a safe slogan only if we understand that it is not prayer itself that has the power, but God. The story of Simon the Sorcerer in Acts 8 is so sobering because it is about a man who wanted to acquire and possess the power of God to do his bidding. This is the danger inherent in separating power from the God who is the source of the power. In prayer there is power because in prayer we know we are in God.

Prayer as Purpose: "We Are for God"

Mission and prayer go together. Whether it is Jesus praying to the Father as a part of the divine mission which was the incarnation or the disciples going out two by two to preach or the modern missionary or businessman seeking to bring the message of the kingdom to people in the world, prayer is the supply line whereby we acquire divine wisdom and strength. When we pray about the concerns of being in the world but not of the world and of being sent to the world, we rehearse the truth that we are here *for God*. Prayer shapes our consciousness of what it means to be ambassadors for Christ; it forms our fundamental sense of identity as believers.

As in all aspects of spiritual development no one on the outside may be able to measure what is growing on the inside, but what we can and must believe is that with a daily bowing before God in attitude and disposition, people are shaped. Prayer transforms us.

The Ministry of Prayer:
One Church's Story

We could linger on the topic of prayer for a very long time. But what we ultimately need to ask is, What should we do with the programs of our churches so that formative prayer will happen?

I have had the privilege of serving at Elmbrook Church for almost twenty years now. Elmbrook Church, like most churches, longs to have prayer as one of its hallmarks. But how does one measure whether a church is "a praying church"? We might decide that a midweek prayer service would be the measure, but that would be purely arbitrary and limiting. We could poll attendees to find out how much they pray, but against what standard would we measure the response? Like those at many churches, the people who attend Elmbrook Church are like the crowds who at various times gathered around Jesus in a set of concentric circles—close disciples, ordinary disciples, followers, and curious crowds. There is no way to measure the spirituality of such a mix, and it's entirely unhelpful to describe an average, because there really is no average.

What we know about Elmbrook Church is that it includes many who have a faithful ministry and lifestyle of prayer, many who long to pray more and pray better, and many who have not yet begun to have prayer as a part of their lives—quite a mix. We know that back in the 1970s the traditional midweek prayer service dwindled in effectiveness and needed to be replaced with small-group ministry where prayer and other ministry functions could be executed more personally and more reliably. We know that during the course of one week, prayer happens in small groups, in families, in

Bible studies, in worship events, in small prayer clusters, in committees, in cars, and in "closets." And we know that we don't really know the measure of it all. What we have done is to teach about prayer as it comes up in classes and sermons, to talk about it in leadership gatherings, and to urge all ministries to incorporate prayer wherever they can.

There are moments when a church can raise the bar on prayer, and one such moment for Elmbrook Church came in 1998. It was the fortieth anniversary of the church, and a grass-roots initiative developed to commemorate the year in some way. The leadership of the church decided to use the anniversary year not just as a celebration and commemoration, but as a call to spiritual renewal within the congregation. A forty-day period was marked out at the beginning of the year, leading up to a grand celebration worship service. We wrote a forty-day devotional book that traced a "Journey with God" from Genesis to Revelation and included daily prayers. We provided a copy for every person in the congregation in seventh grade and older, along with an accompanying CD or cassette filled with forty songs to match the devotional themes. Each night during the forty-day period we held a prayer meeting in the chapel. Each lasted an hour and a quarter and was led by many different ministries and age groups. Each night only a small proportion of the whole congregation attended, but cumulatively there were many different people involved. At each meeting there was dynamic interaction between God and the people who participated.

We urged small groups of the church to use the devotional materials and music that had been distributed. The weekend worship services also used the same themes and music. At the end of the forty days we had a service of celebration—a time of enthusiastic thanksgiving and praise, recollections of God's faithfulness and blessings over the years, and prayers for the future. I will never forget singing "Great Is Thy Faithfulness" at the conclusion of the service—the first verse sung by those who first came to the church in the 1950s, the second verse by those who came in the 1960s, and so on, until the whole congregation belted out the last verse.

God worked in the hearts of many during that season. People wrote about new understandings they had gained, new gratefulness, and new experiences they had received. Nominal believers were moved as well as long-standing, mature believers. Many said they sensed that the attitude of the church in a general, intangible way, had softened. There was a new sense of unity. The long-standing prayer warriors of Elmbrook observed that prayer had made its way into the bloodstream of the church.

Not surprisingly, lots of people wondered how we would continue such a wonderful time. After praying about it and discussing it, the leadership decided we should not institutionalize what had happened, fixating it into a program of the church. Some things that happen are unique; they don't fit into a program. Prayer activity is like that; you can't put incense in a bottle. We concluded that we should be watchful for special opportunities to have seasons of prayer, and always to keep teaching how prayer can be continually present in the lives of individuals and groups.

Prayer and Solitude

We have talked about public prayer because our focus is on the role of the church in spiritual formation. We would be remiss not to address the issue of private prayer, however, because it is foundational.

Almost anywhere in this book we could have raised the issue of solitude, but perhaps it is best associated with prayer. In Latin *solus* simply means alone, and that is the essence of solitude. It is a proper form of isolation or seclusion, a drawing away for a holy purpose.

Solitude nullifies any notion we have that prayer is a matter of show. We may think we know that, but it is all too easy, especially when we think of prayer mostly as a public event, to perform for other people rather than commune with God. Jesus' warning couldn't have been stronger:

> When you pray, do not be like the hypocrites, for they love to pray standing in the synagogues and on the street corners to be seen by men. I tell you the truth, they have received their reward in full. But when you pray, go into your room, close the door and pray to your Father, who is unseen. Then your Father, who sees what is done in secret, will reward you.
>
> Matthew 6:5–6

He talked about those who "for a show make lengthy prayers" and warned that they would be "punished most severely" (Luke 20:47). Prayer in solitude gives undivided attention to God by setting aside any public self-consciousness or pretense that gets in the way.

Solitude also sets aside the distractions of life and practices standing *solus* before God. Jesus sought solitude at critical times and as a part of his normal routine:

> After leaving them, he went up on a mountainside to pray.
>
> Mark 6:46

But Jesus often withdrew to lonely places and prayed.

Luke 5:16

One of those days Jesus went out to a mountainside to pray, and spent the night praying to God.

Luke 6:12

Then Jesus went with his disciples to a place called Gethsemane, and he said to them, "Sit here while I go over there and pray."

Matthew 26:36

One would think that solitude would come easy, but for many of us in the modern world it is as difficult as any other spiritual activity. Silence is threatening (note how common it is for people to have television, stereo, or radio continually on in their homes or cars). To have something noisy happening all the time is to protect ourselves from what might happen if things suddenly got very quiet. Noise prevents us from thinking, and it lets us off the hook in our responsibility to reflect.

In a busy culture of sheer pragmatism solitude looks like a waste of time, or an unjustifiable indulgence. If we, like Jesus, knew that our mission and career would last two or three years, how many days in the wilderness would we spend in solitude?

Promoting Formative Prayer in the Church

So then, how can we foster the practice of prayer in the lives of our congregations without being superficial or mechanical about it? A church can promote formative prayer in a number of practical ways.

Be intentional about how prayer is modeled in public services. Have lay people lead in prayer. Select people whose prayer has a natural and sincere quality. Avoid the cliché. Demonstrate the full range of vital prayer: praise, thanksgiving, supplication, confession, etc.

Teach about prayer. Don't turn every teaching about prayer into a harangue, and don't simply say that if we prayed more the world would be changed. The biblical instruction about prayer is wide and deep, and teaching about it should captivate listeners and leave them motivated to learn more.

Encourage people to bring prayer into all functions of the church. Don't make one prayer event (a weekly meeting, a prayer day) *the* litmus test for whether the church is praying.

Look for unique moments in the church to have a specifically prayer-oriented event or season of prayer.

Be honest about the struggles of prayer. Leaders should admit how they sometimes find it hard to be motivated to pray and talk about where they find dryness, oppression, or hard work in prayer.

Emphasize the privilege of prayer. Help people be awestruck that the Creator of the universe has permitted us to approach him anytime, anywhere. Cultivate an attitude of prayer.

Point people to the Trinity. One of the earliest evidences we have that early Christians thought of Jesus as divine is that some of their prayers were addressed to him. God has revealed himself to us as Father, Son, and Spirit. Revelation of person always has implications for communication. Prayer will be wider and will go deeper when we avail ourselves of the opportunity to address the Father, the Son, *and* the Holy Spirit.

Talk about the practice of journaling as a form of prayer. Encourage people to not merely make lists of requests but to write out heartfelt conversations with God.

Develop prayer chains that connect people in small groups or in a network that goes through the whole church.

Designate leaders who will have a special ministry of prayer to the sick. Encourage those who have special gifts of prayer to focus on that as their ministry in the church.

Offer people the opportunity to have someone pray for them at the conclusion of each worship service. Let the final word in worship be, we will hold you up before God.

It cannot be overstated that prayer forms us and transforms us. This dialogue with God is the direct and dynamic impressing of God's mind on our souls. Our words to him are the overture for his word to encompass and shape our hearts.

Churches must teach prayer as a practice, model prayer as a privilege, and develop prayer as an instinct in every corner of the church's life.

Bending and Serving

Formative Worship

May your Spirit guide my mind, Which is so often
    dull and empty.
Let my thoughts always be on you, And let me see
    you in all things.
May your Spirit quicken my soul, Which is so
    often listless and lethargic.
Let my soul be awake to your presence, And let
    me know you in all things.
May your Spirit melt my heart, Which is so often
    cold and indifferent.
Let my heart be warmed by your love, And let me
    feel you in all things.
                        Johann Freylinghausen (1670–1739)

We must be appalled at the prospect of a Christian attending church worship week after week and not being at all
shaped by it. Yet it happens all the time, in every conceivable kind of church. Is it the church's fault? Perhaps.
Is it the individual's fault? Maybe. It also must be a strategy of the devil, for what is more devilish than whole congregations of people performing duties with legalistic
pride, all the while believing they pay God the high honor

of worship? People end up insulating themselves from the shaping power of the Spirit, and they portray a weak, insipid testimony to the world. This is Christianity? A religion of suits, smiles, and Styrofoam cups?

Worship must be more about God than us. If we enter the sanctuary of worship focusing on the carpeting *we* chose, the pews *we* installed, the songs *we* picked, the musicians *we* pay, the Bible text *we* select, and the communion cups *we* have filled, then worship will be filled far too much with us instead of the Almighty.

The devil likes for us to enter the sanctuary with the same ease with which we enter our recreation rooms and to focus on the same sensory expectations we have when attending a concert. The one thing he doesn't want to happen is for us to meet with God.

Yet this is the essence of worship—meeting with God. We see that in God's walks through the garden with Adam and Eve, in the tent of meeting that was filled with the smoke of God's glory, and in the temple and the synagogue. We learn about worship when we see people worshiping Jesus by bowing down and clasping his feet, and we see worship in the mighty images in Revelation.

Worship as Bowing or Bending

Exuberant definitions of worship abound. But let's consider the two basic definitions given us in the Scriptures. The first is to bow or to bend.

What exactly does it mean when it says that the two Marys worshiped Jesus in the garden of resurrection (Matt. 28:9)? And what about the Magi who worshiped the Holy Child (Matt. 2:11), the disciples in the boat just after Jesus calmed the storm (Matt. 14:33), or the blind man Jesus healed (John 9:38)?

We know that none of them took a guitar out of a case or turned to their favorite hymn. These scenes do not portray offering plates, pulpits, or invocations. Yet they are some of the best passages for helping us to properly use our offering plates, pulpits, and invocations. What happened in those scenes is that awestruck individuals went to their knees, bent down, and even prostrated themselves before the awesome power and majesty of Christ. In the bowing, they worshiped. The bowing *was* the worship—worship is taking one's proper position before the living God. After worship, we are able to respond to God as the creatures that we are. Worship is a complete reorientation and the only sensible way to approach life.

The Gospel writers in these passages draw on a Greek word group that refers to the bending of the knee or bowing low. *Gony* and *gonypeteō*, from the word for "knee," point to this act of worship. Sometimes gestures are merely gestures, and sometimes they encompass the whole meaning of an act. The latter is the case here. Genuflection was common not only in the Greco-Roman world (slave before master, devotees of oriental religions), but also in the Old Testament. The faithful kneel before God out of respect—for example, Solomon before the temple and Daniel three times a day before God in prayer (1 Kings 8:54; Dan. 6:10). God says that every knee will bow before him (Isa. 45:23), a promise echoed and amplified in Philippians 2:10. This gesture is a spiritual act of humility, submission, respect, and dependence.

The story of Hezekiah's revival (2 Chronicles 29–31) is a wonderful picture of worship rediscovered. The spectacular set of scenes begins with cleansing the temple of years of accumulated rubbish and filthy idolatries. Levites stand in the temple's doorway, ready to use cymbals, harps, trumpets, and lyres to lead singing as in the days of David, Gad, and Nathan. Then worship began:

> The whole assembly bowed in worship, while the singers sang and the trumpeters played. All this continued until the sacrifice of the burnt offering was completed. When the offerings were finished, the king and everyone present with him knelt down and worshiped. King Hezekiah and his officials ordered the Levites to praise the LORD with the words of David and of Asaph the seer. So they sang praises with gladness and bowed their heads and worshiped.
>
> 2 Chronicles 29:28–30

They bowed, they knelt down, they bowed their heads—they worshiped.

A second Greek word has a similar sense. *Proskyneō* may have the etymological meaning of kissing, as in kissing the ground in prostration before someone's majesty. Here too is a gesture of homage, deference, and obeisance. In the Septuagint the word is used for bowing before prophet, king, angel, or God (see Gen. 22:5). In the New Testament *proskyneō* is used almost exclusively in the Gospels and almost entirely in reference to bowing before Jesus. The wise men bow (Matt. 2:11) as do Jairus (Mark 5:22), the healed leper (Matt. 8:2), and Jesus' disciples after the resurrection (Matt. 28:17). Each instance shouts out the deity of Jesus, for God alone may be worshiped.

Satan couldn't get Jesus to bow (Matt. 4:9) because for him to do so would turn the universe upside down and reality inside out. In Revelation some bow before the beast and others before God, but ultimately all the nations will worship God alone (15:4). John 4, a text crucial to biblical understanding of worship, finds Jesus explaining "true worship" with the term *proskyneō*.

To worship is to bow. Archbishop William Temple put it this way in his *Readings in St. John's Gospel:*

> Worship is the submission of all our nature to God. It is the quickening of conscience by his holiness; the nourishment of mind with his truth; the purifying of imagination by his beauty; the opening of the heart to his love; the surrender of will to his purpose—and all this gathered up in adoration, the most selfless emotion of which our nature is capable and therefore the chief remedy for that self-centeredness which is our original sin and the source of all original sin.

Simply put, Temple's formula says that worship is submission. Putting a knee to the ground or bending the head signals with the body what is happening in the soul. Temple reminds us that worship does not bend just one part of ourselves before God, but our whole nature. Conscience, mind, imagination, love, will—all of what we are and all of how we function must bow. If Temple is right that this is "the chief remedy for that self-centeredness which is our original sin," then there can be no doubt that worship shapes the soul.

Worship as Service

The second main concept for worship in the New Testament is service, encompassed by two words: *latreuō* and *leitourgeō*. The English word *liturgy* comes from the latter. It can hardly be said that there is a formal liturgy in New Testament worship—the word is not used in that way—but as a word used in the Septuagint for the sacrificial ritual of the tabernacle and temple, there is a ritualistic sense to it.

The word *latreuō* appears throughout Exodus, Deuteronomy, Joshua, and Judges in reference to sacrifices. God insisted that his people serve him and him alone. The way that principle was rehearsed again and again, one generation after another, was through sacrifices brought by all to be prepared and sacrificed by the priests. Fire and smoke, the smell and sizzle of burning fat, blood, water of the great basins for washing—all these images must have made deep impressions on young minds. God had provided salvation through substitution and sacrifice—a terrible price for the great crime of sin—resulting in wonderful absolution. Service of God in worship was participation in the process of salvation. Knowing that it is only by Christ's sacrifice that we are really saved, we must serve God in worship.

Of course, apostasy was evident even in Old Testament days in places where one could go through similar rituals in service to the gods of the Canaanites or others. There has always been true worship and false worship.

The New Testament sometimes uses the word *latreuō* to refer to the Old Testament cultic function. This is especially true in Hebrews (8:5; 9:1, 6, 9, 14; 10:2; 12:28; 13:10). Elsewhere the word refers to aspects of the faithful life such as prayer (Luke 2:37; Acts 26:7) or serving God in ministry (Rom. 1:9; 2 Tim. 2:3). There is an eschatological dimension: "They are before the throne of God and serve him day and night in his temple; and he who sits on the throne will spread his tent over them" (Rev. 7:15). Revelation 22:3 says, "No longer will there be any curse. The throne of God and of the Lamb will be in the city, and his servants will serve him."

Probably the most memorable use of *latreuō* is in Romans 12:1 where Paul speaks of a most comprehensive act of worship as service: "Therefore, I urge you, brothers, in view of God's mercy, to offer your bodies as living sacrifices, holy and pleasing to God—this is your spiritual act of worship *[latreuō]*."

Are We Worshiping Yet?

So what does any of this have to do with the worship service that will inevitably begin next Sunday at your church? What difference does any of this make for the songs we choose, the topic about which we preach, who prays, and when we have people stand and sit?

This is exactly where theory and practice must merge. What good is a theology of worship if it doesn't affect how we worship? The best chance for worship that is truly formative in people's lives comes when the biblical reality of worship is the very atmosphere breathed by the congregation on Sunday morning. Next Sunday, all around the world, Christians will worship—some in English, others in Swahili, Flemish, Amharic, and dozens of other languages. Some will use pianos, others will use organs or flutes or drums. Some will worship for an hour, others for three. Some will whisper, others will shout.

In a refugee camp in Rwanda several hundred of the faithful will meet with God under a tin roof with walls made of UN provided plastic tarps. Sitting on volcanic rock, their *leitourgos* will include a nearly unending string of ebullient native Christian songs. In a village in the Cotswolds of England twenty or thirty people will gather in a quaint stone-walled church built three hundred years earlier. They'll sing the well-metered poetry of their Anglican hymns, and ruminate on the slowly-intoned words of the local vicar. In southern California thousands will gather in an arena-style church, eager to meet with God as the words of Scripture are projected on screens and shorts-clad ushers collect the offering.

All three have one thing in common. They will go away saying that they have worshiped. Are they right? The only proper way to answer that question is to use biblical criteria. Jesus himself gives the measure of worship:

> Yet a time is coming and has now come when the true worshipers will worship the Father in spirit and truth, for they are the kind of worshipers the Father seeks. God is spirit, and his worshipers must worship in spirit and in truth.
>
> John 4:23–24

There is no doubt that the Rwandan, English, and American worshipers previously named all believe that they offer true and spiritual worship to the true and spiritual God. When it comes to views of worship, opinions vary. Some believe that true worship occurs rarely, only when numerous variables are performed just right. They believe that only their way of worshiping is right. Others have a more open-minded view. They have no problem believing that worship is taking place in a variety of circumstances. So how do we know when true worship occurs?

It may help to think of three aspects of worship, ranked in a hierarchy of sorts: purposes, practices, and effects.

The Purposes of Worship

At the top of the pyramid are the purposes of worship. This is most important because worship must always be evaluated against the biblically defined divine intent. Prior to discussion of likes and dislikes, what "draws us close to God," and what it means to "really worship," we must listen to what God says about worship. God wants

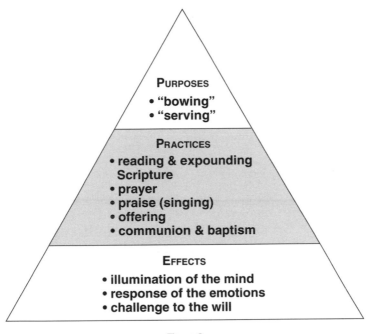

Figure 3
Defining Worship

us to bend the knee or bow before him, and he wants us to serve him. We must trust that that is the kind of worship that will form our souls.

Immediately we see that genuine worship has more to do with heart than form. True worshipers worship in spirit and in truth, and they do so when they are serving God by bowing low before him. Just when does that happen? We bow in submission when we gather offerings and present them out of respect to God, when we listen attentively to the reading of the Word, and when we bow in prayer. We serve the King when we say, "Amen," to a pure-hearted testimony or when we quietly meditate on the Last Supper while participating in the Lord's Supper. If the purpose of worship is submission of the whole self, then every element of a public worship service—not just some parts—can and should fulfill that purpose. Keeping the focus on purpose will help us understand what we are doing and why, and it will allow us to walk away from the Anglican chapel, the Rwandan shelter, or the Californian auditorium saying that we have worshiped the living God.

The Practices of Worship

That brings us to the second level of the hierarchy: the practice of worship. There is a short list of typical worship activities that are fairly obvious to anyone who thinks about worship. When we worship, we pray, praise God in song, read and expound Holy Scripture, make offerings, witness baptism, and participate in the Lord's Supper.

Some churches do other things as well, and the form for each of these things varies. Throughout the ages—from Old Testament times through the intertestamental development of synagogue worship, into the experience of Jesus and Paul, through the early Christian period, across the Middle Ages, the Reformation, and now in the modern period where Christianity has come to more culturally distinct groups than ever before in history—these fundamental activities of worship remain the same. Their historical and cultural transcendence comes not from simple convention or mindless conformity, but from biblical authenticity. When believers gather to worship, they instinctually know that they are to do these things.

Knowing what we are to do when we worship allows us to believe in and take assurance from the *objectivity* of worship. Well-meaning Christians sometimes agonize over whether or not they are really worshiping, answering the question based on the subjective effect worship has on them. We sometimes believe that we have really worshiped only when we feel joy, sense the presence of God, or are moved to a greater level of affection or action. While we cannot deny that these are good and desirable effects of worship, we must not use them to measure worship.

Sometimes we don't feel as though we've worshiped because we have not gotten enough sleep or are grieving a major loss. We might not feel as though we've worshiped because the preacher's presentation was hampered by the stomach flu, or because the guitarist chosen for the weekend didn't know how to tune his strings. Such things may distract the worshiper, but they do not prevent worship.

Precisely for these reasons it is important to keep the *purposes* of worship foremost in our minds, then commit to engaging the biblical and historical *practices* of worship "in spirit and in truth." Then we will say, "Thank you, God, for allowing us to worship you today." To do so puts us together with believers throughout history— the priests of the temple who had good days and bad days of making animal sacrifices; those Christians who worshiped quietly in the cramped catacombs; isolated Christian families in modern Muslim lands whose worship is a private family moment; hospice-bound believers who have the Bible read to them and share communion alone with their pastors; and brand-new churches meeting in school gymnasiums and fumbling with songsheets, dim overhead projectors, and metal folding chairs.

Believing in the objectivity of worship allows us to get beyond our hesitations and doubts. It assures us that we can be anywhere in the world and find the means to worship. When people claim they have found a church in which they can worship only after years of searching, what are they saying has been happening in the meantime? Is it really possible that God has cast that person adrift, withholding from him or her the basic tools of worship? Is God content to not be worshiped while we look around for a place and a people where we can enjoy worship? And what about people who live on the back roads and hidden valleys of the world—those who do not have multiple churches from which to choose? It can't possibly be true that real worship can happen only when we have just the right combination of variables, variables inaccessible to people living in most places.

It's not wrong to seek the best worship setting that can be found in a given situation. A benefit of denominationalism is its allowance for one faith to be expressed and experienced in different forms. The reason to emphasize the objectivity of worship is simply to ensure that we don't equate the meaning and essence of worship with human experience. God wants spiritual beings to realize their spirituality, not to worship it.

We might ask ourselves what would need to happen in our place of worship for God to be able to say, "I was worshiped here today." This refreshing way of thinking about worship focuses on God rather than us. Focus is important. Try to seek romance for romance's sake and the whole thing is really about one person. Try to experience worship for the experience's sake and God is relegated to second place in our minds.

So what does it take for God to be able to say "I was worshiped"? The biblical answer would seem to be when believers seek to fulfill the *purposes* of worship through the wonderfully constant *practices* of worship to the end that we experience the *effects* of worship.

The Effects of Worship

Finally, we get to the last section of the pyramid, the effects of worship. These are the subjective experiences of worship that both happen during the act of worship and endure beyond it. Its place at the bottom of the pyramid does not indicate that it is least important, but that it is the logical and chronological result of a sequence starting with purpose.

Placement at the broadest portion of the pyramid reminds us that experience is often what the congregation is most aware of. We may want to think that most of the people ponder the purpose of worship, relish the endurance of time-honored activities of worship, or focus on the qualities of true worship. In fact, though, much or most of the time what we think about is how a worship event affects us. That said, it is perfectly proper to understand, to seek, and to cultivate a rich experience of worship. Joy and peace as the consequence of being right with God are good.

Through worship all of who we are is shaped. The effects of worship are illumination of the mind, waking of emotion, and challenge to the will. Worship ought to cause people to say,

"I now know something I didn't know before."

"I have sensed the holy presence of God and my lowliness before him; I have a joy that can come only from him."

"I better comprehend that God is in charge of the universe."

"I know I need forgiveness; and I know I need to forgive."

"I long to follow Christ more closely, to be shaped by him so that I can represent him faithfully in the world in which I live. I desire to obey what I have heard from his Word this day."

"I can see that I am a part of his holy community. I am not better than anyone else, nor am I less worthy than anyone else. I am in the midst of a people who need to throw themselves on God's mercy, and who need to come back again and again to bow before him and serve him."

Practical Steps to Planning Formative Worship

What then can we do to take the resources we have and cultivate a worship environment that is faithful to worship's purpose and is formative in people's lives? Here are some suggestions:

Remind the congregation of worship's purpose. They may come looking for joy or relief or a sense of belonging. Don't begrudge them that, but do them a great service by orienting them to bow before and serve the King right from the start of a worship service.

Teach about worship. Whenever a biblical passage describes a worship scene, draw out the dynamics of what happened. Apply to worship biblical exhortations to adore and submit to God.

Avoid showmanship in worship. Solos need not be homely nor sermons unpolished. Excellence can coexist with genuineness. But avoid seeing the worship service as a string of acts. That is the surest way to distance worship leaders from the congregation.

Consider the variety of people who respond in different ways to different styles of worship, but remain committed to the core principles of worship.

Train worship participants (music leaders, pray-ers, technical personnel, etc.) to think in terms of embracing the whole congregation. Remind the worship team that the event of worship is not happening on the platform, but in the whole room—side to side, front to back. A few people on the platform don't cast a worship product back into an audience. Every living, breathing body in the room has come before God. We're in it together, and worship will happen with the community gathered or it won't happen at all.

Include predictable and unpredictable elements in worship. Predictable elements allow people a sense of continuity and confidence; unpredictable elements demonstrate the dynamic nature of worship and its expansive possibilities.

Be creative without being esoteric.

Have more than one person plan the worship service. Use teamwork. Don't break the worship service into a series of territories. If preacher, musicians, and others can't cooperate on planning worship, how can they lead the congregation in unified worship?

Bring the fruit of the Spirit—love, joy, peace, patience, kindness, goodness, faithfulness, gentleness, self-control—into both the planning of worship and worship itself.

Worship can and should be a church's greatest moment. There is no event in earthly experience like a human community serving God with humbled, bowed hearts and minds. Worship is a perpetual series of transformational moments, and the habit of worship one of our best chances for genuinely changed lives.

To Know and to Be Known

Formative Fellowship ————————

> I love thy Church, O God! Her walls before Thee
> stand,
> Dear as the apple of Thine eye, And graven on
> Thy hand.
> Beyond my highest joy I prize her heav'nly ways,
> Her sweet communion, solemn vows, Her hymns
> of love and praise.
>
> Timothy Dwight (1800)

Fellowship and Spiritual Direction

The fellowship of the church is that most remarkable phenomenon where all of our talk about the importance of the Christian community becomes a practical reality for transformation.

Some traditions and churches emphasize one-on-one connections. "Spiritual direction," "mentoring," and "discipling" are some of the terms used to describe the intentional pairing of individuals for a program of spiritual growth. A mentor acts not as a therapist, not as a general counselor, but as a spiritual advisor who listens and provides spiritual guidance as a mature, objective party.

The advantage of such arrangements is that individuals receive individual attention. That direction, however, is only as good as the faithfulness, wisdom, and integrity of the mentor. Christians must remember that while they may have leaders they follow and exemplars they emulate, they should not really be disciples of anyone except Jesus.[1]

A person may find spiritual direction in a network of supportive relationships. Mutual study, prayer, and accountability with a number of different peers and mentors wonderfully fulfills the ideal of fellowship in the body of Christ.

One of the most extraordinary developments in the modern church is the small group movement. Churches of widely divergent denominational, ethnic, and nationalistic backgrounds have embraced this form of ministry because it is so effective in many ways. Weekly home Bible study, for example, is a natural setting for prayer, worship, study, counsel, accountability, service, and evangelism. Place believers in such an environment, and many of these happen almost instinctively. The wisest proponents of the small group movement see it not as a modern innovation, but as the renewal of a respectable and time-tested form of ministry. They link it with such models as the house churches of the New Testament, the Moravian societies, and the Wesleyan class meetings. This allows us to benefit from the lessons of history and heightens our level of confidence in this form of ministry. More important, at the heart of small group ministry is *koinonia* or fellowship. We may be tempted to think of fellowship as something very ordinary, an event symbolized by coffee cups, living rooms, and chit-chat. But fellowship is a deeply spiritual experience by which members of the body of Christ meet, join together, and experience God's presence in a new way.

Spiritual formation happens in, with, and through fellowship. The day-to-day, shoulder-to-shoulder contact of believers with other believers shapes us. Sometimes contact is a grinding experience where sparks fly and sharp edges are worn off; other times it is more forming and fitting. Whatever the case, fellowship influences. I often reflect on three different fellowship groups in which I have been privileged to participate at various times during the past twenty-six years. In each instance I belonged not for weeks or months, but for years. In each case the group became like my family; they accepted, encouraged, guided, challenged, prayed for, supported, and questioned me. They showed me what the church is. I will never forget their faces. I am eternally in their debt.

The Meaning of *Koinonia*

We're told the early church "devoted themselves to the apostles' teaching and to the fellowship, to the breaking of bread and to prayer" (Acts 2:42). The first Christians devoted themselves to fellowship for many reasons. Their spiritual instinct told them it was a good thing to be together to share the graces of the Spirit and live out what the apostle Paul years later would describe as the life of the "body" of Christ. Member joined to member—interdependent, connected, complementing, supporting—fellowship is one of the great mysteries of God's work. It only happens, though, if there is a real coming together. When that happens, we are shaped by each other, and as such, fellowship is a basic tool in the task of spiritual formation.

The Greek term *koinonia* is rendered in English translations in various passages as "fellowship," "participation," "sharing," "partnership," and "communion." Elements of *koinonia,* such as sharing material goods, sharing in ministry, and being partners in the gospel, are rooted in the spiritual reality of a connection between believers that is based on their connection in Christ. John put it this way:

> We proclaim to you what we have seen and heard, so that you also may have fellowship with us. And our fellowship is with the Father and with his Son, Jesus Christ. . . . If we claim to have fellowship with him yet walk in the darkness, we lie and do not live by the truth. But if we walk in the light, as he is in the light, we have fellowship with one another, and the blood of Jesus, his Son, purifies us from all sin.
>
> 1 John 1:3, 6–7

To understand the significance of human fellowship we must first appreciate the spiritual dynamic of fellowship with God. Various apostolic voices in the New Testament comment on this point. In the passage just quoted, John depicts this *koinonia* with God as the realm and the manner of one's walk, counterposed with a lifestyle that participates in darkness. Fellowship is, in other words, coexisting in the same domain, thereby sharing the same experience and being influenced accordingly. The implication for human beings is clear: Fellowship with light is to be purified and shaped by the light; fellowship with darkness results in degradation and corruption. Paul puts it this way: "Do not be yoked together with unbelievers. For what do righteousness and wickedness have in common? Or what fellowship can light have with darkness?" (2 Cor. 6:14).

Jesus' Gospel statements do not use the word *koinonia,* but the concept is evident in his statements about our unity with him:

> I am the vine; you are the branches. If a man remains in me and I in him, he will bear much fruit; apart from me you can do nothing. If anyone does not remain in me, he is like a branch that is thrown away and withers; such branches are picked up, thrown into the fire and burned. If you remain in me and my words remain in you, ask whatever you wish, and it will be given you.
>
> John 15:5–7

Second Peter 1:4 says that believers may "participate *[koinōnoi]* in the divine nature and escape the corruption in the world caused by evil desires." This is one of the strongest statements in the New Testament regarding the connection of human beings with God. To share in the divine nature does not mean that humanity becomes divine, but that humanity is restored to its divine likeness through spiritual formation.

The apostle Paul also speaks forthrightly about *koinonia* with God and between believers. What better picture of this do we have than the sharing of the bread and the cup—communion of Christian with Christ and with other Christians. As Paul puts it:

> Is not the cup of thanksgiving for which we give thanks a participation *[koinonia]* in the blood of Christ? And is not the bread that we break a participation *[koinonia]* in the body of Christ?
>
> 1 Corinthians 10:16

The Lord's Supper is spiritually formative in that it is a perpetual experience of connection and participation. We cannot help but be shaped by this remarkable act in which we rehearse and experience the taking in of Christ as he taught in John 6. This is *koinonia* with Christ, and it is *koinonia* between believers. One loaf and one cup provide a focused experience *with* Christ and a unified experience *between* believers. Our identity with Christ is heightened as we identify with other believers, and vice versa. Through *koinonia* with Christ formative work occurs in the whole body of Christ.

Material *Koinonia*

The mosaic floor of one fourth-century church portrays a deacon holding a basket of bread, pitched forward, almost running to deliver a gift of shared bread to those who could not gather with the rest of the assembly. The whole church should share this same eagerness. Such giving is spiritually formative for both the giver and the recipient.

Paul was simply thrilled by the spirit of fellowship among the Macedonian Christians who "urgently pleaded with us for the privilege of sharing *[koinonia]* in this service to the saints" (2 Cor. 8:4). What service? In this case it was material generosity. They gave out of their poverty, "as much as they were able, and even beyond their ability"(v. 3). Because of it, Paul says, "men will praise God for the obedience that accompanies . . . your generosity in sharing *[koinonia]* with them and with everyone else" (9:13). He urges the Corinthians likewise to "excel in this grace of giving" (8:7).

A simple thing? A passing affection? No! The spirit of fellowship evidenced in material generosity cuts against human nature as we experience it in the world. The greedy, acquisitive, self-preserving impulses in humanity are so great that whole theories of history are based on them. The materialist says material competition is the driving force of history, thereby dismissing the notion that people and churches could be motivated by altruistic generosity.

Familial sharing and occasional acts of generosity do exist in the world, but a natural flow of generosity is to be the hallmark of the body of Christ. Something supernatural happens there—something formative. The Macedonian spirit of sharing may take many forms: meals delivered for a week following a funeral, a collection taken for a family strung out by unemployment, gifts sent to a missionary.

Material *koinonia* speaks volumes, but it comes out of the greater reality of the spiritual connections between believers.

Fellowship and Self-Disclosure

Sharing fellowship prompts people to unveil themselves to each other and produces the potential for profound, lasting spiritual formation. Fellowship is knowing and being known. For the most part we long for these things because we need them so desperately. An easy way to answer the question of whether you are in fellowship is to ask if you know others and are known. Ask if there is at least a small circle of people you know better now than you did a year ago. And question if there is a group of people who know you better today than they did a year ago. If you are in fellowship through regular, natural, honest relationship, and if you take the opportunity to disclose the struggles, needs, advances, graces, and failings of day-to-day life, then mutual comprehension flows quite naturally.

This is what people mean when they say that their Bible study group or their small group is like a family. It's the reason they will pick up the phone the moment a crisis comes up and ask for the prayers of these people whom they know and are known by. It is why they will confess sin in that circle and perhaps nowhere else.

A discipline is involved here. The unveiling of selves ordinarily does not happen quickly. Crisis can strip people down to their true selves and cause them to coalesce around the mercy of God. An intensive experience such as a ministry trip can immerse people in the personal lives of others. But ordinarily the best outcome of fellowship happens with gradual, progressive, mutual comprehension. Fellowship is not measured in days or weeks, but in years or even decades. When a church's leaders have gotten to know each other as colleagues in ministry over the long haul, they can finally reach a point where approaching decisions is made easier by the familiarity of history.

The unveiling of the self is a high risk. Everybody knows that, and we learn strategies for minimizing that risk. Some people don't mind the risk and may actually divulge too much too soon to too many people. That is not a measure of good fellowship, though. Under normal circumstances, people progressively open up in an environment where they trust they will not be taken advantage of or abused.

Such an environment requires a good theology of God's grace and truth. People must believe that they stand before a God from whom no secret can be kept and that they stand in a fallen human community with the potential to be redeemed by God. Then they can venture out under the protective umbrella of God's truth and love.

Class Meetings, Then and Now

The genius of the eighteenth-century Methodist movement under John Wesley was multi-faceted: gospel preaching, social action, strategic organization, lay mobilization, and others. One of the movement's fundamental building blocks was really a mature expression of fellowship—the class meeting. Working with people in the Church of England, Wesley saw the need for a structure alongside the local parish to care for the spiritual activities of the movement's adherents. Methodist societies were precursors of Methodist churches; but the societies were broken down into smaller groups, the so-called class meetings that in many ways formed the backbone of the movement.

Consider the similarities between these meetings and modern small group ministry: weekly meetings, about a dozen members, led by qualified leaders, engaged in Bible study and prayer. The class meetings constituted a vital formative influence for their members.

Class meetings did differ from the modern small group in one way. They were designed to be probing cells of accountability. Members were not only allowed to confess to one another, they were practically compelled to do so. Consider one description of these challenging meetings:

> There they sat, twelve persons "having the form and seeking the power of godliness"; in the center, on the plain table, the leader's Bible; around it, the circle of chairs, each with its occupant. Generally the leader pitched the tune for an opening hymn. . . . Followed prayer, fervent, from the heart, that the Spirit of God might be present, to expose the inmost thoughts and imaginings, and to inspire all to new heights of living, and after that the reading of a passage of Scripture, with perhaps a running fire of commentary from the class leader. "Brother Watson," the leader would demand, the reading done, "how has it been this week with your soul?" Stammeringly, the lad from

the farm just outside the village would rise to his feet. Words would not seem to come. At last, with a mighty wrench, "I thank the Lord, well," he would mumble, and sit down. But the old leader was not satisfied. "Praise the Lord," he would encourage, and then the probe would go in. "No wrestlings with temptation?" "Yes." The lad's head might hang, but there was never any thought of holding back an answer. "Did that old temper rise up again?" "Yes." "And did you win the victory?" "Yes, thank God." "Hallelujah, Brother Watson. Go on as you are and one day the crown incorruptible will certainly be yours." [singing] "I the chief of sinners am, But Jesus died for me." And the circle would take up and carry to its end the familiar stanza.[2]

The author goes on with further descriptions, then closes: "So the conversation passes around the circle. It is doubtful whether in all the record of religious gatherings since the days of the apostles there has been such an instrument for personal upbuilding as this."[3]

In *The Story of American Methodism*, Frederick Norwood says,

Always central was the idea of close personal fellowship which could be achieved only in a small group. This is where the class meeting comes in. If ever the society or local congregation became too unwieldy, at least in the class meeting intimate community could be maintained. Ideally, no more than twelve would be together under a class leader to meet weekly for spiritual guidance, prayer, Bible study, individual witness, and discipline. Everyone would know, in close personal terms, everyone else. The class leader would be familiar with the personalities of each individual and his situation in life, including his family background and business relations. In the typical class, persons of different ages and stages would be together—old, young, men, women, beginners and those going on to perfection.[4]

In 1853 Mr. James Finley related his first exposure to a Methodist class meeting. He came, at the urging of his wife, with a reputation of being a reprobate, one who in the past would not "show [his] ill-breeding and vulgarity by disturbing a worshiping assembly." He continues:

> The leader, as is customary on such occasions, opened the speaking exercises by relating a portion of his own experience, in which he spoke feelingly of the goodness of God to his soul. After this he spoke to the rest in order, inquiring into their spiritual prosperity: addressing to them such language of instruction, encouragement, or reproof, as their spiritual states seemed to require. It was a time of profound and powerful feeling; every soul seemed to be engaged in the ranting, incoherent declarations which I had been told they made on such occasions, I never heard more plain, simple, Scriptural, common-sense, yet eloquent views of Christian experience in my life. After all the members had been spoken to the leader came to me, and in a courteous, Christian manner, inquired into my religious condition.[5]

Such was the pleasant surprise of someone we wouldn't even call a seeker in modern parlance.

What words can we use for the richness of fellowship when it works well? Is it too much to call it a wonder? A miracle? A mystery? Apparently the apostle Paul was awed at the divine intent that in Christ "the whole building is joined together and rises to become a holy temple in the Lord" (Eph. 2:21). The outcome is not merely theoretical, it is real: "And in him you too are being built together to become a dwelling in which God lives by his Spirit" (v. 22). It is why God took the trouble to bestow on the church apostles, prophets, evangelists, pastors, and teachers, "to prepare God's people for works of service, so that the body of Christ may be built up until we all reach unity in the faith and in the knowledge of the Son of God and become mature, attaining to the whole measure of the fullness of Christ" (4:12–13).

The *koinonia* enjoyed by the first Christians who met in houses in Jerusalem, the Moravian assemblies, the Wesleyan class meetings, the modern Chinese house churches, and the serious home Bible study group today, represents the potential for a gospel community that not only authenticates the metaphor of the body of Christ but represents one of the best hopes for personal spiritual formation.

Formative Fellowship

Churches today experiment with *koinonia* in every conceivable way: men's groups, women's groups, support groups, senior citizens groups, gatherings of coworkers, teachers, neighbors, single parents, young mothers. It's not hard for a church to promote fellowship, either through small groups or other forms of ministry. But what must happen for these ministries to have a transforming effect on their adherents? What qualities were core to the historical success stories?

Formative Fellowship Requires Leadership

It is generally not difficult to get people to enjoy social contact. Gathering with a regular group, becoming familiar with each other, and enjoying mutual support is wonderful, but to be formative, fellowship must stretch further. Leaders so often make the difference. A leader can't guarantee that formative fellowship will happen, but with no leadership or misdirected leadership, fellowship is limited. A small group leader, for instance, will set the tone, move the agenda, and challenge members. Social groups left to themselves will chart some kind of course, but they will not direct themselves toward a spiritual goal. That's the purpose of Christian leadership.

There is no one model for a fellowship leader. God uses a wide variety of temperamentally diverse leaders to produce serious fellowship. Good leaders display a positive, expectant attitude about fellowship. They view every gathering as a work of God in progress, and they expect something to happen. They see even homely little groups as fronts where the Spirit can intervene. They believe the time and effort to prepare and plan is worthwhile. They resist the temptation to let the group coast.

Such leaders develop over time. They need to be recognized within the church and given freedom to make mistakes along the way. They need training, and can learn from others who have been doing the same thing for a longer amount of time.

Formative Fellowship Requires Modeling

People in the church need to be convinced that the risk of engaging in fellowship holds great promise. They are more likely to take the risk if they see leaders modeling fellowship and hear testimony of others regarding the crucial difference fellowship has made in their lives. Pastors must communicate how fellowship experiences have been formative in their own lives.

Though it can be complicated, people need to find a venue in which they are truly engaged in fellowship.

Leaders of a church can validate fellowship by making visits to groups a high priority. Church leaders must view an evening spent with a dozen people in a home as strategic as anything else they do during the week.

Often testimonials given in a worship service or other large group focus on the experience of the individual with God, but we should deliberately identify people who can testify to the grace they have experienced through community. That signals everyone that they must be fully connected in fellowship. Let people speak about how their small groups rallied around them when they lost a loved one, when a fire took their home, or when they went through depression. It will invite others who aren't in fellowship to come across the threshold.

Formative Fellowship Requires Good Theology

Theological propositions, often unspoken, can either bolster or undermine fellowship. Consider the following:

	Weak Theology (undermines fellowship)	Good Theology (bolsters fellowship)
Triune Existence of God	God only appears to be a Trinity.	God really is a Trinity who mysteriously includes community within himself.
Definition of the Church	The church is an association of people who believe in and desire the same things.	The church is a community connected by the dynamic movement of the Spirit and headed by the living Christ.
Definition of Salvation	Salvation is the one-time rescue experience of individuals.	Salvation is the process of a people being rescued and transformed.

continued on page 110

continued from page 109

	Weak Theology (undermines fellowship)	Good Theology (bolsters fellowship)
Work of God	God only works immediately upon individuals.	God sometimes works immediately but most often mediately through the body of Christ.
Roles in the Church	Gifts and roles in the church distinguish believers from one another.	Gifts and roles in the church form bonds within it.
Purpose of the Church	The purpose of the church is to accomplish tasks God has set out.	The purpose of the church is to be the quality of people God desires and to do what he requires.
Goal of the Church	The goal of the church is to urge people to accept Christ.	The goal of the church is to make disciples, the starting point of which is accepting Christ.

The quality of our fellowship ministries is affected by the quality of our theology. It's our understanding of who God is, how salvation works, and what he wants the church to be, that will define the form and depth of our fellowship.

Formative Fellowship Requires Trust

Fellowship is an ongoing workshop in faith. Church leaders need to believe that if they encourage fellowship groups to flourish in the church, this does not represent a lack of control and something that is likely to cause splits in the church. Fellowship should not, therefore, be limited to carefully constricted programs with no latitude for development. Some of the best new ideas for ministry and initiatives to reach out to the community come from the free, creative activity of small groups

The Dynamics of Spiritual Formation

in the church. Faith in Christ's power to work through his church allows us to give each other the freedom to fail. We learn through mistakes, and there is a huge difference between small messes and major disasters. Church leaders need to let the church enjoy fellowship, and to oversee fellowships not from a distant sentry point, but by being in fellowship with them.

Formative Fellowship Requires Time

As we discussed earlier, the notion of growth, spiritual or otherwise, assumes progressive formation over time. This is God's chosen way. *Koinonia* takes time. It takes time for a church to figure out how it can offer *koinonia* to its members, to teach the principles, and to model the benefits. It takes time in any given fellowship group for people to develop a truly personal knowledge and trust of each other. Time marches us through hard times and calm times—there is no crash course in fellowship, no expedited life of community faith. It takes time to make enough small mistakes and enjoy enough small successes to process what we are learning.

Formative Fellowship Requires Focus

Intimate subsets of the church can accomplish much of what the church is to be and do, but they are not able to do it all. For example, a Bible study group is not the basic unit for world evangelization strategy or the full worship ministry of a church.

The small group that meets regularly with more or less the same constituency can focus on some basic activities of spiritual growth: prayer, study of the Word, worship, and service. Such groups can evaluate themselves on an annual basis to see how they are doing in each area, then work out the imbalances, and encourage group members in the pursuit of challenging goals such as service.

A whole church can focus on the function of caring. Shepherding the flock—feeding, protecting, caring—necessitates individual attention, and the only way that will happen is if there are a multitude of individuals ready with words and acts of compassion, discernment, and direction. Small groups are the best vehicle for personal care in the church. Pastors and other church leaders should be grateful for the continual care-giving that occurs there. Most of it never becomes public. Much of it is even subconscious because we don't continually, consciously think about living within the realm of someone else's love and care. Nonetheless, it is real.

The first disciples did not merely exhibit fellowship, they were "devoted" to it. *Koinonia* will not happen automatically. That is why it has been absent in many chapters in the life of the church. On the other hand, fellowship isn't a mountain summit achieved only rarely and with great effort. Given the right theological understanding of who we are and what we are about as the church, and with the willingness to step out and risk, the spirit of *koinonia* that produced spiritual transformation for the primitive church will prompt the same for us.

The Shaping Word

Formative Preaching

O Creator of the universe, who has set the stars in the heavens and causes the sun to rise and set, shed the light of your wisdom into the darkness of my mind. Fill my thoughts with the loving knowledge of you, that I may bring your light to others. Just as you can make even babies speak your truth, instruct my tongue and guide my pen to convey the wonderful glory of the gospel. Make my intellect sharp, my memory clear, and my words eloquent, so that I may faithfully interpret the mysteries which you have revealed.

Thomas Aquinas (1225–1274)

The Nature and Importance of Preaching

It is hard to believe that there ever would be questions about the importance of preaching and teaching the Word in the ministry of the church, but there are. Those who fear authoritarianism, irrelevancy, or traditionalism raise objections to preaching. Some even argue that modern people have such short attention spans that they cannot possibly be expected to listen to a string of words that exceeds eight or nine minutes. Some church leaders uncritically accept that proposition as dogma.

After decades of preaching around the world and witnessing the effects of preaching, John Stott makes the following comments:

> If it is true, as Jesus said, endorsing Deuteronomy, that human beings do "not live on bread alone, but on every word that comes from the mouth of God" (Mt 4:4; Dt 8:3), it is equally true of churches. Churches live, grow and flourish by the Word of God; they wilt and wither without it. The pew cannot easily rise higher than the pulpit; the pew is usually a reflection of the pulpit.

> What, then, does it mean to worship God? It is to "glory in his holy name" (Ps 105:3), that is, to revel adoringly in who he is in his revealed character. But before we can glory in God's name, we must know it. Hence the propriety of the reading and preaching of the Word of God in public worship, and of biblical meditation in private devotion. These things are not an intrusion into worship; they form the necessary foundation of it. God must speak to us before we have any liberty to speak to him. He must disclose to us who he is before we can offer him what we are in acceptable worship. The worship of God is always a response to the Word of God. Scripture wonderfully directs and enriches our worship.[1]

Most people are not indifferent about preaching. They may love it, loath it, aspire to it, follow it, reject it, trivialize it, criticize it, respect it, avoid it, or seek it. If they hear sermons, they will have a reaction. Many well-known historical figures have voiced their own opinions about preaching:

> Martin Luther: "A preacher must be both soldier and shepherd. He must nourish, defend, and teach; he must have teeth in his mouth, and be able to bite and fight." "A preacher should have the skill to teach the unlearned simply, roundly, and plainly; for teaching is of more importance than exhorting."

> Abraham Lincoln: "I don't like to hear cut-and-dried sermons. When I hear a man preach, I like to see him act as if he were fighting bees."

> Phillips Brooks: "Preaching is truth through personality."

> D. Martyn Lloyd-Jones: "To me the work of preaching is the highest and the greatest and the most glorious calling to which anyone can be called. If you want something in addition to that I would say without any hesitation that the most urgent need in the Christian Church today is true preaching."[2]

> Edgar DeWitt Jones: "The preacher for this day must have the heart of a lion, the skin of a hippopotamus, the agility of a greyhound, the patience of a donkey, the wisdom of an elephant, the industry of an ant, and as many lives as a cat."

> St. Francis de Sales: "The test of a preacher is that his congregation goes away saying, not what a lovely sermon, but, I will do something!"

> Dietrich Bonhoeffer: "For the sake of the proclaimed word the world exists with all of its words.

In the sermon the foundation for a new world is laid. Here the original word becomes audible. There is no evading or getting away from the spoken word of the sermon, nothing releases us from the necessity of the witness, not even cult or liturgy . . . The preacher should be assured that Christ enters the congregation through those words which he proclaims from the Scripture."[3]

Richard Cecil: "To love to preach is one thing—to love those to whom we preach, quite another."

John Newton: "My grand point in preaching is to break the hard heart, and to heal the broken one."

Austin Phelps: "Genius is not essential to good preaching, but a live man is."

Preaching is standard equipment for spiritual formation. Justin Martyr, writing in the middle of the second century, tried to explain the unusual practices of the Christians to a pagan audience:

And on the day called Sunday, all who live in cities or in the country gather together to one place, and the memoirs of the apostles or the writings of the prophets are read, as long as time permits; then, when the reader has ceased, the president verbally instructs, and exhorts to the imitation of these good things.[4]

Similarly, the North African writer Tertullian explained:

We assemble to read our sacred writings . . . With the sacred words we nourish our faith, we animate our hope, we make our confidence more steadfast, and no less by inculcations of God's precepts we confirm good habits. In the same place also exhortations are made, rebukes and sacred censures are administered . . . [5]

So where does skepticism about the ministry of preaching arise? Should we blame the purveyors of postmodernism who have pronounced that teaching principles is archaic, who say that interpretation of ancient texts can and should only be the subjective experience of the reader?

On the one hand we can be glad that the postmodernists have rejected the modernist dissection of the Bible. On the other hand, we must be disturbed when truth is viewed as entirely relative. Surely postmodernism has raised doubts about the foundations of preaching: the original text, the process of interpretation and application, the possibility of universal meaning.

We may not have parishioners quoting authors and artists who promote postmodernist ideals, but a trickle-down effect shows up in the congregation sooner or later. When people ask for "good stories," they may simply want us to bring the Bible to life for them so they can comprehend it, or they may be saying that the only meaningful way to communicate biblical principles is through stories. The former is a proper goal for preaching; the latter is not.

In truth, though, modern philosophies are not entirely to blame for the weakening voice of the pulpit. Sometimes churches lock preaching in a back closet. They are threatened by it just as God's people avoided the interventionist words of the prophets in the Old Testament. Some preachers have bored churches to sleep. Churches try to tame preachers, and the next generation wonders about the relevance of quaint preaching. Preachers let pride and privilege turn preaching into weekly power plays. Self-conscious intonation, fashionable dress, intellectual prowess, prestigious titles, and celebrity status become a game that holds the fascination of some star-struck parishioners and is rejected by others. Preaching represents immense power and potential for incredible good or pervasive, long-term damage: "The tongue has the power of life and death" (Prov. 18:21).

The Goal of Preaching

What is the measure of fruitful preaching? There are many short-sighted ways to answer that question: Are the people pleased? How many compliments have people given? Are they listening well? Are they showing an interest in cassette tapes of the message?

The temptation to use such measuring sticks arises from our natural human desire to be accepted and liked. But surely we know that what really matters is whether people are genuinely encountering God through his Word in a way that forms their lives. This can't be measured in a few weeks or months of preaching, but over the long haul. Here again we may come back to Ephesians 4 for a reminder of the long view of Christian ministry:

> It was he who gave some to be . . . pastors and teachers, to prepare God's people for works of service, so that the body of Christ may be built up until we all reach unity in the faith and in the knowledge of the Son of God and become mature, attaining to the whole measure of the fullness of Christ.
>
> verses 11–13

These are words of long-term, progressive spiritual ministry: "to prepare," "until we all reach," "become mature," "attaining the full measure." We know that ministry of the proclaimed word is central to it all. All of this work is to the end that

> we will no longer be infants, tossed back and forth by the waves, and blown here and there by every wind of teaching and by the cunning and craftiness of men in their deceitful scheming. Instead, speaking the truth in love, we will in all things grow up into him who is the Head, that is, Christ.
>
> verses 14–15

The teaching ministry of the church is aiming at growing up people into Christ. The alternative is dreadful: to be carried along by the winds and waves of any of a multitude of human-generated philosophies of life. Such people may feel like they are buffeted by these influences. They may be quite comfortable in what seems to them like the mainstream of society while the secure shoreline of the Christian gospel appears as the sharp edge of destruction.

It takes time and love with good instruction to educate a child, and it takes the same to bring Christ into the core of people's being. The preacher/teacher is a shepherd in the fullest sense of the word, carrying out basic, life-giving shepherding functions:

feeding—giving the sheep the spiritual nourishment that will enliven their souls

leading—knowing the direction the sheep should be going and directing them accordingly

protecting—watching for the wolves and the precipices that claim the lives of sheep

Formative Prospects of Preaching

What, then, spells the difference between preaching that merely fills allotted time and that which shapes the inner and outer lives of people?

Preachers Must Believe in What They Preach

Preachers may come to the pulpit confident that they have enough notes to fill the time, enough but not too many illustrations, a catchy introduction and a snappy conclusion—but not having let the Word sink deep into their own hearts. We sometimes think our task is to get a grip on the text before Sunday morning, but what needs to happen is for the text to get a grip on us. A sermon is not a well-prepared and elegantly presented meal we serve up to the congregation. It's a translation and delivery of an urgent message of truth and grace that God has already shouted at us. It includes words of comfort, warning, explanation, guidance, encouragement, and correction. It addresses issues that touch on all of reality: the nature of God and the dynamics of marriage, the beginnings of the universe and the organizing of personal priorities; the mission of the Spirit of God in the world and the decision we make about loved ones on life support; the meaning of life and the mode of baptism; the thoughts of God and the emotions of the human heart. If the ministry of preaching and teaching is the transmission of the truth of God contained in the Word of God, then the range of application and the power of the One who is behind it makes the formative possibilities staggering.

Someone has said that there is hardly anything more powerful in human interaction than one person standing before a group of people to say, "This is what I believe." Proponents of religion, philosophy, or even salesmanship recognize this truth. People believe what they have heard someone boldly proclaim as personal belief. Christian proclamation includes much more than a personal statement—a body of Holy Scripture, a validating historical record, and contemporary testimony. But we must not ignore the importance of preachers believing what they preach before they preach it. Preachers must offer conviction, not merely conjecture; authority, not merely consensus; truth, not merely opinion.

"My heart is held captive by the word of God" were Martin Luther's words when he stood before the emperor and the Diet of Worms in 1521 to explain why he would not take back the controversial writings he had penned. It was early in the Reformation movement, but the principle was already firm. The word itself is the authority of God, and we are not to shape it; it must hold us captive. We should carry this image into the pulpit.

We can trust the long-term effects of biblical preaching. Like a farmer sowing seed, we don't go looking for an immediate harvest. We must believe in the inexorable process whereby the planted word will take root and bear fruit (depending of course on the soil in which it lands).

Preachers Must Be Authentic

This principle balances the previous. Preachers must believe what they preach and they must present it authentically. Otherwise, people will have ample reason to hold the preaching and the preacher at arm's length.

The word *authenticity* has become commonplace in church lingo today. For some, the concept is that of

Christian leaders spilling out their own shortcomings, struggles, and failings. Authenticity means more, however, than the preacher making sure that somewhere in the sermon there is a moment of attention-getting self-disclosure. This kind of public confession can get mechanical, predictable, and powerless. Authenticity—the quality or condition of being authentic, trustworthy, or genuine—does include self-disclosure. More than that, though, it is a complete stance of honesty in the preaching process.

Once when I was a teenager I took a non-believing, skeptical friend to a Christian meeting where I was sure he would hear the truth. Because he was a thoughtful person, I was confident he would respond to what he heard. When I asked him what he thought, he replied, "Words, words, words." My heart sank. His response may have just been conveniently dismissive, but it convicted me. Whenever and wherever possible, we must proclaim the Word with as much disarming genuineness as is possible. Never should we compromise the Word by stacking words upon words that are only a house of cards.

Authenticity joins truth and authority. Truth is more than the sum of truths. The expression "the true God" (e.g., Jer. 10:10; 1 John 5:20) indicates that God is the real God, the genuine God. So his truth is "the real deal." The Christian messenger says: "This is reality—a true picture of the world the way it really is, you the way you really are, and God the way he really is. Believe this because it will help you live your life in reality."

Honesty in preaching begins during the preparation process as we submit to the authority of the Word, relying on God to resist tendencies to twist or shape it into something we deem more portable, useful, or palatable. With this approach the emerging sermon forms our thinking instead of the opposite.

Genuineness emerges when preachers are in full contact with the Word they are preaching. The preacher says, "Just look what I've found here," and is not hesitant to say where the Word has had a saddening or gladdening effect.

Preaching Must Translate

Preaching is translation, carrying a message across a distance. Preaching should enter people's heart. Otherwise there is not a chance it will be formative.

In his superb book about preaching, *Between Two Worlds,* John Stott said:

> This earthing of the Word in the world is not something optional; it is an indispensable characteristic of true Christian preaching. . . . Our bridges too must be firmly anchored on both sides of the chasm, by refusing either to compromise the divine content of the message or to ignore the human context in which it has to be spoken. We have to plunge fearlessly into both worlds, ancient and modern, biblical and contemporary, and to listen attentively to both. For only then shall we understand what each is saying, and so discern the Spirit's message to the present generation.[6]

The preacher is indeed a bridge-builder or translator, bringing the eternally true Word of God into the world in which people live. If the preacher prefers the Word and ignores the realities of the world in which people live, whether out of indifference, super-spirituality, or laziness, then the preaching will not make contact with the issues and concerns of people's lives. If, on the other hand, the preacher is only concerned about contemporaneity, then there is a real risk that the biblical content of the preaching will be thin and watery.

How often we have let bad examples of preaching dissuade us from what is truly possible. We hear wooden presentations of Bible doctrine that put people to sleep or prompt unthinking nods, so critics claim we cannot preach Bible doctrine in the modern world. We hear sermons that are largely compilations of commentary from magazines and newspapers, and we conclude that we must denounce all attempts to contextualize the message. We end up tempted to wander in the middle, somewhere in the never-never land of platitude and sentiment, with no real contact with either the world of biblical truth or the societies in which we spend our days.

Spiritual formation occurs through the ministry of preaching when the word of the Spirit is steadily, carefully translated to the personal and social issues facing both the preacher and the listeners.

Formative Preaching Is More Than Relevant

The word *relevance* is frequently used when speaking about effective preaching. Relevance means, for one thing, to be related or connected to another. When applied to preaching, it describes the principle that preaching must touch people's lives.

Preaching must be relevant; it must connect. When we think about spiritual formation, however, relevance doesn't tell the whole story. It is not just that we want the Word of God to come alongside or touch the issues of people's lives—we want it to *enter* their lives. Christian preaching, like other means of spiritual formation, aims to enter into the consciousness of believers. This assimilation is more likely if the preacher aims at the hearts and souls of listeners. We are not on our own, though, to figure out a map that will navigate us to that inner sanctum of the human heart—that is precisely what the Word of God itself does.

In Colossians we find a wonderful expression about the formation of Christ in the heart:

> Let the peace of Christ rule in your hearts, since as members of one body you were called to peace. And be thankful. Let the word of Christ dwell in you richly as you teach and admonish one another with all wisdom, and as you sing psalms, hymns and spiritual songs with gratitude in your hearts to God. And whatever you do, whether in word or deed, do it all in the name of the Lord Jesus, giving thanks to God the Father through him.
>
> Colossians 3:15–17

The peace of Christ *in* the heart; the Word *dwelling within*—these are ways of describing an experience that goes to the core, a true assimilation of the divine Word. As the means of this experience, preaching acts as one of the greatest tools of spiritual formation in the church.

Preaching to the Core

But what is the core at which preaching should aim? Should preaching aim at the characteristics that distinguish different kinds of people living in different kinds of situations? In modern times there is a great deal of attention given to the things that make human beings different: age, gender, social class, ethnic background, temperament, nationality, philosophical persuasion. There is no question that there is a marvelous diversity in creation that shows up in the human race. It is also plain to see that sin has caused differences to turn into divisions and rifts in humanity. It is a great challenge to cast the Word of God into this sometimes tangled web of humanity.

There is another way of looking at preaching. Instead of being concerned primarily with the places where people are different, we may choose to aim at the heart. When we do, we speak to the universal core of human experience. People sometimes complain that a sermon has gone over their heads, but they can never complain that it went too deep into their souls.

The Expended Life

Formative Service

> Give unto us, O Lord, we humbly beseech thee,
> a wise, a sober, a patient, an understanding, a
> devout, a religious, a courageous heart; a soul full
> of devotion to do thee service; strength against
> all temptations.
>
> William Laud (1573–1645)

Someone has compared the open, generous life to the
Sea of Galilee, and the closed, selfish life to the Dead Sea.
These two bodies of water in Palestine are connected by
the Jordan River in a direct north-south line along the
Great Rift Valley. Clear, sweet water from underground
springs flows into the Sea of Galilee. In turn, the Sea of
Galilee flows south into the Jordan. Galilee is a gorgeous,
active lake, full of life that has sustained fishermen in the
region for millennia. The Dead Sea, by contrast, is a shallow, selfish basin with no outlet. It hoards the water that
flows into it. Some water evaporates, leaving behind
brackish, clouded water so dense that swimmers bob like
corks. The whole sea is dead.

Service is an issue of spiritual formation because the believer who is not serving is like spiritual backwater, inevitably limited in how much life he or she can contain. The ministering believer lives out the very meaning of grace. Service is not just an issue of external appearances; it is not about busyness and sweat. It is fundamentally an issue of the soul, and what happens on the outside is directly linked with what is happening on the inside.

Rediscovering Service

It's hard to exaggerate the difference between the Christian who has discovered service and is doing it, and the one who doesn't have a clue. The issue is not that one is busy and can list practical accomplishments and the other cannot. There is a difference in the quality of faith, the frequency of joy, and the depth of understanding of God and his ways.

Many Christian leaders have noted the practical, tangible rediscovery of the priesthood of all believers in the local church as one of the most encouraging things that has happened in the modern era. More and more churches enthusiastically teach that the gifts of the Spirit are widely distributed, the call of God to service is universal, and the opportunities for serving are immanent if we are open to the breadth of possible ministry. Instead of limiting ministry to worship leadership on Sunday and tasks such as visitation, funerals, and weddings, the modern church asks a question: Why should we not release people into a wide array of functions—some public, others private, some extraordinary, others mundane— and affirm that to serve Christ in any way is to be genuinely human?

The Biblical Meaning of Service

As we consider the meaning of service, let us first note what service is *not*. It is not mere external activity, and it certainly is not using our hands to make our hearts right. It hardly seems we should have to make such statements, but centuries of experience in the church have taught us that we often stand one short step away from works-righteousness. The believers Paul addressed in Galatians were bewitched by it. The earliest recorded sermon outside the New Testament, called Second Clement, is infected with it. The church has repeatedly passed through the cycle of slipping into works-righteousness and then rediscovering the gospel of grace.

The hardest words Jesus spoke to anybody at anytime were a condemnation of the spirit of self-righteousness:

> Woe to you, teachers of the law and Pharisees, you hypocrites! You give a tenth of your spices—mint, dill and cummin. But you have neglected the more important matters of the law—justice, mercy and faithfulness. You should have practiced the latter, without neglecting the former. . . . You clean the outside of the cup and dish, but inside they are full of greed and self-indulgence. Blind Pharisee! First clean the inside of the cup and dish, and then the outside also will be clean.
>
> Matthew 23:23, 25–27

It's not easy to give up Phariseeism. It can be so useful. As Christian leaders we can be tempted to keep just a bit of the spirit of the Pharisees in the church so that people will do things we want them to do, even if out of a sense of spiritual pride or anxiety. But despite its appeal we must expunge such self-righteousness.

The polar opposite of works-righteousness, complete spiritual passivity, is not, however, a better alternative.

Too often believers have avoided works-righteousness by doing no work at all. To favor passivity over work may be a simple exchange of hubris—taking away the pride of activism only to replace it with the pride of gnostic spirituality. This is a disconnection from the active, vibrant movement of the body of Christ. It contradicts many biblical mandates, including the basic description of ministry in Ephesians 4 that says leaders are "to prepare God's people for works of service, so that the body of Christ may be built up" (v. 12). Jonathan Edwards pointed out that we are not saved on account of our works, but we are not saved apart from works. Dallas Willard has said that the opposite of grace is not effort, but merit.

Service, *diakonia*, is at the heart of the mission of Christ: "For even the Son of Man did not come to be served, but to serve, and to give his life as a ransom for many" (Mark 10:45). Some New Testament passages depict Jesus as the fulfillment of the Old Testament suffering servant passages. The church, as the body of Christ, is to take this same posture. Here lies a paradox, though. If Christians think of the church as a service industry organized and outfitted to serve their needs, the church will be impotent. Yet the members of the church are indeed called to serve God by serving each other in the church (as well as serving those outside), and so the church is the best place in the world to receive the benefits of service. In *The Freedom of a Christian,* one of his pivotal treatises, Martin Luther makes one of his typically paradoxical statements: "A Christian is a perfectly free lord of all, subject to none. A Christian is a perfectly dutiful servant of all, subject to all."[1] Herein lies the radical freedom of a Christian.

Paul said there are "different kinds of service" (1 Cor. 12:5). He was thankful that he was appointed to Christ's service (1 Tim. 1:12), and he frequently mentioned his fellow workers (e.g., 2 Cor. 8:23).

Ephesians 4 says that works of service build up the body of Christ because they are the means whereby individual believers discover where they fit. It begins with finding one's life in Christ and continues with the community-building work of the Spirit who joins all individuals together: "And in him you too are being built together to become a dwelling in which God lives by his Spirit" (Eph. 2:22). Like the stones of the temple, quarried and dressed for a holy purpose, Christians are placed side by side, being the dwelling of God and performing the service of the temple of God. But how does this work practically?

Moving People toward Service

In one respect, getting people to serve is one of the hardest things we try to do. It asks people to go against the grain of fallen human nature: be selfless; give precious time, energy, and money; risk comfort. On the other hand, people who discover service often experience a kind of epiphany. They find a joy and genuine spiritual contentment that comes only after the expenditure of real effort with right motives and proper expectations. Service gets in their spiritual bloodstream and, as long as they don't mismanage themselves into bitterness or burnout, they may serve in the church for a lifetime.

The church must provide opportunities to serve. Church leaders need to apply their spiritual imaginations, let go of the need to control, take some risks, and allow for there to be a few messes. Leaders must have enough faith to believe the church will not be defamed if someone tries a new form of ministry that later proves to be unfruitful. Perfectionism in the church is bondage. Leaders need to find ways to say "yes" rather than assuming that the answer should almost always be no. Someone once said they had a nickname for overly-restrictive leaders in their church. They called them "danger-is" people because their response to most fresh ideas was, "but the danger is . . ."

We need to use an appropriately wide, biblical definition of service. Speaking of worship, Paul told the Colossians, "And whatever you do, whether in word or deed, do it all in the name of the Lord Jesus, giving thanks to God the Father through him" (3:17). Then a few sentences later, he adds: "Whatever you do, work at it with all your heart, as working for the Lord, not for men, since you know that you will receive an inheritance from the Lord as a reward. It is the Lord Christ you are serving" (3:23–24).

In a local church, that "whatever" can include dozens of different activities. Some go back as far as the first century, others are entirely contemporary. All are interpreted, performed, and acknowledged as *diakonia:*

ushering	greeting at the door
counseling	administrating
singing in choir	teaching children
cleaning floors	setting up chairs
leading Bible study	chairing a committee
publicizing an event	praying for the pastors
visiting the ill	maintaining the church's web site
directing traffic in the parking lot	counting the offering
selling tickets for a concert	acting in a church drama
escorting newcomers to classes	teaching a pre-baptism class
leading music in worship	sewing costumes for an Easter play
getting involved in foster care	volunteering in soup kitchen
leading chapel service in nursing homes	stocking pews
cooking meals for shut-ins	selling cassette tapes
organizing the church library	assisting with bulk mailings
setting up communion	sponsoring a refugee family

coordinating weddings	training Sunday school teachers
offering lay counseling	serving on a missions committee
writing to and praying for missionaries	editing the high school ministry newsletter
reading Scripture	
interpreting worship services for the hearing impaired	volunteering as a youth camp counselor
visiting prisons	

Service and Spiritual Formation

The serving believer will be transformed through serving. Ill motives—pride, self-righteousness, fear, competition—can mess it all up, but barring such incongruities, service will shape the soul.

Service draws the Christian closer to Christ as he or she senses the privilege of acting on his behalf. Service produces a sense of purpose that is eternal, even while grounded in the earthly and physical needs of those being served. Humans need a sense of significance, and being with and acting on behalf of Christ makes us sense something even larger than significance.

The sense of being a part of something so much larger than yourself is a soul-stretching experience. Soldiers on the battlefield, astronauts on the launch pad, and Olympic athletes marching with their countrymen experience this sense of being caught up in something larger than themselves. For the Christian it is even more exciting. You are part of something not just larger than yourself, but larger than your church, larger than the worldwide Christian community, larger than the world, the universe, and time itself. To be a servant of the living God is to be part of the unfolding of reality itself. To serve God in the church is to see a bit of the fulfillment of "thy kingdom come, thy will be done, on earth as it is in heaven."

What should Christian shepherds do to help service be a formative experience? Prepare people to take their first steps. Give instruction on the purpose and mindset of Christian service. Provide a context in which people can process what they experience in service; they will surely have bumps and scrapes along the way. Help people assess what they are learning about themselves and about God through their serving. And always look for the long view; we are not looking to get people involved only in occasional projects, but to encourage a lifestyle of service.

I'll never forget the scene in our church the night before we opened our brand-new sanctuary. The carpenters, painters, and other contractors had finished their work just hours earlier. Tools were being packed up, electric cords rolled up, and the local building inspector had just issued an occupancy permit after his final inspection (just twenty-three hours before the dedication service!). The place was a mess. About two hundred volunteers descended on the building with vacuums, dust rags, brooms, and other cleaning supplies. Many were teenagers. My wife and I brought our children and set them to work wiping down wooden molding. I hoped they would remember the excitement of such an extraordinary night of service. More important, I hoped that when it came their turn to help in the nursery, greet at the doors on Christmas Eve, serve as teen helpers in the Sunday school, or take any other opportunity for service, they would not consider it a chore but a joy. I wanted them to consider service as normal a thing to do in the community as anything else, and to see that it is a direct communion between them and Christ.

The priesthood of all believers is not merely a theory; it is to be the normal activity of normal Christians. *Diakonia* is a translation of effort into devotion.

Metamorphosis

The Final Goal

> Most holy and eternal God, lord and sovereign
> of all the creatures, I humbly present to thy divine
> majesty, myself, my soul and body, my thoughts and
> my words, my actions and intentions, my passions
> and my sufferings, to be disposed by thee to thy
> glory; to be blessed by thy providence, to be guided
> by thy counsel; to be sanctified by thy Spirit; and
> afterwards that my body and soul may be received
> into glory; for nothing can perish which is under
> thy custody, and the enemy of souls cannot devour,
> what is thy portion, nor take it out of thy hands.
>
> Jeremy Taylor (1613–1667)

Change as Metamorphosis

There is perhaps no more dramatic description of the
prospect of change in the New Testament than the word
transformation. Metamorphosis in Greek, the word elicits
memories of biology class where teachers first describe
the remarkable process whereby tadpole becomes frog,

caterpillar emerges as butterfly, and maggot turns to fly. One dictionary defines metamorphosis as "change in form or structure, as if by magic or sorcery."

On numerous occasions my children have placed a chrysalis they found in a terrarium so that they could witness for themselves the spectacle of metamorphosis. Only a fortunate person gets to watch a caterpillar attach itself to the underside of a twig, twist and turn to pull a covering up and over itself, and then cease to move at all and enter dormancy. With the passing of weeks it seems that the chrysalis has turned into a sarcophagus as there is no evidence of life whatsoever. Then, one day a crack opens and what emerges is something that would be the most bewildered creature on the face of the earth if it had self-consciousness. The old has gone, the new has come! There is no resemblance to the old, and the former way of behaving will no longer work. It takes a while before the creature's wings unfold, but if you try to assist it, the butterfly will die. Finally, with one flap of the wings, it is gone on the wind. It is a transformation as complete and astounding as can be and a symbol that Christians have used for the resurrection life of Christ for centuries. It reminds us that transformation is the work of God. A caterpillar cannot become a butterfly by behaving like one. Nor can butterflies give butterfly lessons to caterpillars. People cannot change themselves, and spiritual leaders cannot do it for them.

The idea of metamorphosis is woven into our culture in stories and legends (e.g., *Beauty and the Beast, Dr. Jekyll and Mr. Hyde*), endless children's games, and toys. It's there in classical literature as well. In Aupuleius's *Metamorphoses* (known since Augustine's time as *The Golden Ass*), a man turned into an ass is saved only by a metamorphosis prompted by the goddess Isis. The story pictures the Hellenistic religious ideal of change, one that is far from the Christian notion of transformation.

Some stories about metamorphosis reveal a fear that change can be regressive. Franz Kafka's famous short story "The Metamorphosis," written in 1915, has a young salesman awake one day to find that he has been transformed into a hideous insect-like creature. At first, his altered behaviors are a curiosity as he scurries along the floor. But soon he is banished and rejected by his own family, which results in his slow slide into despair and death.

The issue of transformation transcends metaphors and stories that give no more than approximations. When we speak of metamorphosis, we are really talking about real change: in attitude, in spiritual knowledge, in ethic, in the way we relate to other people, and in character.

Some think dramatic change is out of the question, usually because the experience of long years has taught them so. With Jeremiah, they raise the question: "Can the Ethiopian change his skin or the leopard its spots?" (Jer. 13:23). Others take a more naïve position, believing that anyone can change simply by turning over a new leaf or by force of will. The Christian answer lies between the hopeless and the naïve. Belief in the possibility of metamorphosis comes directly from the promise of God and the life-changing power of the Spirit. But how much transformation can we actually expect to see in people?

Most Christian traditions expect real transformation but preserve the concept of incremental growth. John Owen (1616–1683), who was pastor, chaplain to Oliver Cromwell, Dean of Christ Church, Oxford, and considered by many the greatest Puritan theologian, once said, "Raise your expectations of what Christ can do for you." This he wrote at the end of one of his hard-hitting treatises on sin, speaking of its mortification in the life of the believer. There is hope for transformation, for vigor and power in the spiritual life, but only as we direct our expectations to Christ, encountering his tenderness and faithfulness, and expecting the power of his death and resurrection to conform our spirits. Owen points out that the Holy Spirit alone does this work of mortification:

> First, the Holy Spirit clearly and fully convinces the heart of the evil and guilt that needs to be mortified. . . . Second, the Holy Spirit alone reveals to us the fullness of Christ for our relief. . . . Third, the Spirit alone establishes the heart in expectation of help from Christ. . . . Fourth, the Spirit alone brings the cross of Christ into our hearts with its sin-killing power. . . . Fifth, the Spirit is the author and finisher of our sanctification. . . . Finally, in all the soul's relationship with God, we have the support of the Holy Spirit.[1]

John Wesley understood salvation as "a deliverance from guilt and punishment, by the atonement of Christ actually applied onto the soul of the sinner now believing on him, and a deliverance from the power of sin, through Christ formed in the heart."[2] Wesley preached real sanctification, but his main point was always that faith is the only path to holiness, not self-fabricated moralism. Transformation happens by way of faith and the powerful love of Christ in the heart.

What then, is the role of the shepherd in promoting transformation? If it is the love of Christ that transforms all of us, Richard Baxter says, then that is the finest and most effective offering the pastor may present to the congregation in the interest of their formation:

> The whole of our ministry must be carried on in tender love to our people. We must let them see that nothing pleaseth us but what profiteth them; and that what doeth them good doth us

good; and that nothing troubleth us more than their hurt. We must feel toward our people, as a father toward his children; yet, the tenderest love of a mother must not surpass ours. We must even travail in birth, *til Christ be formed in them.* They should see that we care for no outward thing, neither wealth, nor liberty, nor honour, nor life, in comparison of their salvation.[3]

Christ Formed in Us

Let us consider some of the scriptural foci that speak to the issue of form: the form that God has set out as the distinctly human pattern, how the human form relates to the form of Christ, and how metamorphosis is both a present and an eschatological reality.

Out of the anguish that filled the apostle Paul as he thought about and wrote to the Galatians comes this expression: "My dear children, for whom I am again in the pains of childbirth until Christ is formed in you" (4:19). The verb Paul uses is *morphoo,* a most unusual way to describe inner change. The apostle labors and travails because he sees something good being borne within the Galatians, their life in Christ. There is also, however, the temptation to add obedience to the law to the simplicity of faith. The prospect of metamorphosis for the Galatians consists of the formation of Christ in them, almost like seeing a new life gestating in the womb.

Whether Paul means "in the individual" or "in the community of faith," the point is that the apostle will settle for and longs for nothing less than the formation of the life of Christ within believers.

Elsewhere Paul speaks of Christ in us and we in Christ. The transformation is not simply a person becoming a different kind of person, but a person becoming like

Christ. Salvation is a radical identification with Christ. Submitting entirely to him is a kind of death to self and rebirth as a Christ-person. "I have been crucified with Christ and I no longer live, but Christ lives in me. The life I live in the body, I live by faith in the Son of God, who loved me and gave himself for me" (Gal. 2:20).

The apostle Paul was familiar with personal transformation. A self-righteous Pharisee who pitted himself against the cause of Christ with vigor became a great representative of Christ and one who told the world about him. If ever there was a picture of metamorphosis, Paul's life is it.

To best understand what is meant by the formation of Christ in us we must look at the biblical passages that speak of the form of Christ.

The Form of Christ

The New Testament sometimes describes the mysteries of the person of Christ in terms of his nature *(morphē)* and the form he adopted in the incarnation to become the formal link between heaven and earth. Philippians 2:6–7 says,

> Who, being in very nature God *[morphē theou],*
>> did not consider equality with God something
>> to be grasped,
> but made himself nothing,
>> taking the very nature of a servant *[morphēn
>> doulou],*
> being made in human likeness.

The well-known Philippian hymn includes this remarkable description of the purpose and form of the incarnation of Christ. The Son of God existed with God, as God. The "form" of God is the complete set of characteristics or attributes that make him God. The form of a servant, which is "human likeness" is likewise the essential being of humanity. In other words, while "form" can mean outward appearance, it can also mean the essence of a thing, which is how it should be taken here.

In his book *The True Image: The Origin and Destiny of Man in Christ,* Philip Edgcombe Hughes says that if we want to know what humanity was intended to be, we need to look at Christ:

> The doctrine of man (anthropology) can be truly apprehended only in the light of the doctrine of Christ (christology). Not only the destiny but also the origin of man involves a profound relationship with the Second Person of the Holy Trinity. Indeed, mankind's destiny in Christ is precisely the fruition of mankind's origin in Christ. . . . Man's destiny, implicit in his origin, is the attainment of "the complete knowledge of the Son of God," which coincides with his becoming "the perfect man," his arrival at "the measure of the stature of the fulness of Christ" (Eph. 4:13). Christ, accordingly, is the True Image in which man was *formed* at creation and into which by the reconciling grace of re-creation fallen man is being *transformed.* [italics added][4]

Christ is not the approximation of divinity, nor is he merely like humanity. He is the form of God and the form of man. Thus the incarnation is the final answer to the question of whether the temporal, sensible world stands apart from the spiritual, divine world, or whether the latter touches and transforms the former.

Eastern Christianity places a special emphasis on this. The Greek fathers thought of the incarnation of Christ as the realm of God's saving power. The death of Christ on the cross is certainly a saving sacrifice, but when the Word became flesh salvation had already begun. As John Chrysostom put it:

> He became the Son of Man, though he was the Son of God, in order that he might make the sons of men children of God. In truth, to mingle the high with the low works no harm to the honor of the high, but raises the lowly up from its very humble estate. Accordingly, this is also true in the case of Christ. He in no wise lowered his own nature by this descent, but elevated us, who had always been in a state of ignominy and darkness, to ineffable glory.[5]

In all of this are many reminders that the process of spiritual formation in the life of the believer is from beginning to end the work of God, not the shaping of life by human effort. We had nothing to do with the form or essential being of God, nor did we determine the form of humanity as it first appears in the created order. It was entirely God's initiative that in the incarnation the Word took the flesh and form of humanity. What Christ did during the time of his incarnation on earth was entirely of his design. Metamorphosis happens only with the application of God's power.

Transfiguration, Resurrection, Transformation

The first use of the word metamorphosis in the Gospels occurs in the account of Jesus' transfiguration.

> After six days Jesus took with him Peter, James and John the brother of James, and led them up a high mountain by themselves. There he was transfigured [metamorphōthē] before them. His

face shone like the sun, and his clothes became
as white as the light.

Matthew 17:1–2

This unique moment stands without teaching or detailed explanation. Its significance is self-apparent. This metamorphosis of the one who already had metamorphosed into the *morphē* of humanity was a sign of the divine and eschatological power and glory of his person. Moses' face had been radiant from what he had experienced. The radiance of the transfigured Christ proceeded from who he was, and the disciples were left with the imprint of his power. Though he had emptied himself of his divine position, he had not been divested of divine identity or power. Moments like the metamorphosis on the mountain were signs of this truth.

After the resurrection, Jesus' external appearance changed at his will. Disciples saw him and did not recognize him (Mark 16:12). He suddenly appeared in rooms with locked doors. He appeared in Galilee and in Judea. In it all the disciples witnessed firsthand the power of God to form and transform.

Predestined to Be Conformed to the Likeness

After the ministry, death, resurrection, and ascension of Jesus, the apostles preached a gospel of change. They called for a kind of change that is not merely a slight alteration or dressing up of human nature, but rather utter transformation. Another of the words containing *morphē* occurs in the description of salvation in Romans 8:29:

> For those God foreknew he also predestined
> to be conformed *[symmorphous]* to the likeness of
> his Son, that he might be the firstborn among
> many brothers.

This being "formed with" the likeness *(eikōn)* of Jesus is the return to Eden that is described in so many ways in the New Testament. Formally created in the image or likeness of God and later misshapen and twisted by sin, human beings need to return to the *morphē* of Adam. It is the new Adam, Jesus, who is both a picture of that perfect humanity and a savior who can make it happen: "And just as we have borne the likeness of the earthly man, so shall we bear the likeness of the man from heaven" (1 Cor. 15:49), and "We, who with unveiled faces all reflect the Lord's glory, are being transformed into his likeness with ever-increasing glory, which comes from the Lord, who is the Spirit" (2 Cor. 3:18).

The importance of spiritual formation is this: that it is the predestined intent and plan of God. Not an afterthought or an augmented spiritual activity, transformation is the salvific process.

The Choice

Why is it that we so often quote Romans 12:2?

> Do not conform any longer to the pattern of
> this world, but be transformed *[metamorphoō]* by
> the renewing of your mind. Then you will be able
> to test and approve what God's will is—his good,
> pleasing and perfect will.

Perhaps we keep coming back to this verse because it is one of the clearest statements of our choice in the process of sanctification and spiritual reformation. Two ways are clearly, unambiguously, and boldly identified. We may conform to a pattern defined by the world or one designed by God. The results are radically different. Either way, we are formed according to an exterior pattern. We are not autonomous and self-determined. We will be shaped, one way or another.

The world has a definite pattern. In it the self is deity or shapes its own deity. The appearance and passions of the body take on paramount importance. The creature is worshiped instead of the Creator. And because of all this, a person's motives, aspirations, commitments, and achievements are limited. Yet this is the normal formation of the typical person. The verb translated "conform" means to be shaped by, or to live after a certain kind of pattern.

In popular culture to "get in shape" means to go to the gym, to "be in great shape" is to get a good report from the doctor, to "shape up" one's life may merely mean to get organized or to secure one's financial portfolio. To conform is thought to be a sign of weakness. The conformist is the chameleon or lemming, letting someone else determine one's course of life. Conforming violates the principle held most dear by the modern world: self-determinism. All the while, however, the reality is that people are conforming according to a pattern of this aeon, unless they are being conformed to the shaping influence of God. The real choice is not whether or not to be conformed. We are by nature malleable creatures. The issue is who will be the shaper.

Paul offers a divine alternative: Be metamorphosed. This patterning process is different because the original pattern is different and its source is utterly different. This is the heart of spiritual formation—the intentional, sustained re-patterning of a person's life after the pattern set out by God when he created human beings in his image, but made possible only by divine transforming power. Every miracle of transformation in the Old Testament or in the life of Jesus is not a magic trick or divine razzle-dazzle, but rather the unveiling of his unique divine power to shape and reshape any element of the cosmos. Fishes and loaves may be multiplied, withered hands restored, dead eyes opened, a lake's surface made solid, a cloud shaped into a pillar, corpses enlivened. In each instance God signals, "I can transform anything in the universe I have formed."

The phrase "renewing of your mind" points to the reconstitution of human nature. "Renewing" implies going back to an original pattern, and "mind" points to the very core of the inner life, the workshop where motives, values, decisions, and beliefs are formed. Part of the honor of being created in the image of God is that our nature goes deep. There is a mind at the core. But as surely as twisted minds are the reason for acts of thievery, jealousy, infidelity, genocide, and every other form of sin, so it takes a reshaping of the mind to move toward godly acts.

So Romans 12:2 is indeed not a passing comment. It is a charter of sorts that focuses not on accumulated human achievement, but on the clear choice of who or what forms us.

Assurance of Metamorphosis

Ask a child what he or she learned in school today, and you might get a response of "nothing." Hearing that day after day could discourage a parent unless he or she realizes that the child is learning. Children are often unaware of the incremental, unremarkable steps involved in education, but this is the nature of growth. Daily differences in height measurement will be unimpressive, the daily growth of one's retirement fund may be imperceptible or even negative. These processes need to be seen from the long view.

Paul indicates that spiritual growth is that kind of process as well:

> And we, who with unveiled faces all reflect the Lord's glory, are being transformed into his likeness with ever-increasing glory, which comes from the Lord, who is the Spirit.
>
> 2 Corinthians 3:18

Sometimes transformation is rapid and startling, as in moments when one emerges from crisis, experiences an epiphany, or makes a new commitment. Members of Christ's church should expect extraordinary times of being filled with the Spirit—by the Spirit, for the Spirit's purposes, and in the Spirit's time.

But growth of character is normally an incremental process. Prejudices die slowly. Hearts are gradually softened. Love is a trained affection. Yet Paul promises that we "are being transformed." Steadily, progressively, constructively, we are being transformed. The apostle clearly wanted his audience to be encouraged by this promise. Moses met with God on Mt. Sinai, and his veiled face reflected the Lord's glory. How much greater is the reality that we reflect the Lord's glory not with veiled faces but with transformed faces.

The Christian life is to reflect the character of Christ. A bride's face lights up as she arrives at her groom's side, reflecting the glory and awe of the moment. Likewise, the face of the Christian is character representing character, for the face is the physical presentation of personality and soul.

Form of Death, Form of Resurrection

In his poignant letter to the Philippians, written during desperate moments when he thought his life might be sacrificed at any time, Paul contemplated the form of death and the form of resurrection that was his hope. What more complete proof do we need of the transforming Christ than to see a man face his own demise with an unshakable belief that in resurrection he would be formed according to the *morphē* of Christ:

> I want to know Christ and the power of his resurrection and the fellowship of sharing in his sufferings, becoming like him *[symmorphoō]* in his death, and so, somehow, to attain to the resurrection of the dead. . . . But our citizenship is in heaven.
>
> And we eagerly await a Savior from there, the Lord Jesus Christ, who, by the power that enables him to bring everything under his control, will transform *[metamorphoō]* our lowly bodies so that they will be like his glorious body.
>
> Philippians 3:10–11, 20–21

In every respect, then, the Christian is committed to an unequivocal, unambiguous program: to be shaped according to the image of Christ who is perfect God and perfect man. This program involves contemplation and imitation not only of Jesus' life, but also of his death and resurrection.

What did Paul actually think becoming like Christ in his death meant? It was not the means of death that Paul particularly wanted to imitate, but the sacrificial character of Christ's death. In Paul's mind, his own suffering in prison (and the whole preceding ordeal of opposition, arrest, trial, and everything else he endured as an apostle) had a certain shape. It was not meaningless, random suffering, but sacrifice for a divine cause. Paul knew that in such fashion he was the witness of the saving death of Christ and would be in line with all the other martyrs from biblical times and beyond. This is the core meaning and the power of the martyr's death: sharing the form of Christ's death. The connection with our daily life is found in Jesus' words:

> If anyone would come after me, he must deny himself and take up his cross daily and follow me. For whoever wants to save his life will lose it, but whoever loses his life for me will save it.
>
> Luke 9:23–24

This distinctive "form" of life is possible only through metamorphosis, because the sacrificial life cuts against so many fundamental human instincts. Self-preservation, self-determinism, self-absorption, and self-aggrandizement are stripped away. Becoming like Christ in his death (in death itself and in daily life) and taking one's own cross (self-sacrifice, not random suffering) is the most radical thing a human soul can do. A caterpillar's metamorphosis begins not when the chrysalis opens, but when the chrysalis is formed. This "death" and entombment allows the transforming process to begin. Likewise, for the Christian, becoming like Christ in his death by taking up one's cross is the moment and the method for metamorphosis. Is there another way? Jesus couldn't have made it clearer: "Anyone who does not take his cross and follow me is not worthy of me" (Matt. 10:38).

These are words that come to my mind not when I visit someone in the hospital, but when I'm praying for a young family about to set out for the first time to the mission field. Or when I hear someone say they intend to be patient in a very unsatisfying marriage. Or when

I hear of a businessman being rejected because he refuses to be unethical in his dealings. These people are taking the crosses of self-relinquishment daily with no guarantee that they will receive a tangible reward.

On the other side of this most radical notion of discipleship through self-sacrifice is the equally radical promise of personal metamorphosis represented in the final resurrection: "Christ . . . will transform our lowly bodies." The form of Christ's death is countered by the form of his resurrection. The extremity of these two realities—pulled into death to self, then pulled out into resurrection life—is itself the utter reshaping of a life. Such a process can only be described as transformation.

Practical Implications for the Ministry of the Church

The local church should offer neither more nor less than this: intentional plans and programs of spiritual formation that seek to bring people to the transforming power of God, which is the ordinary way of salvation in sanctification.

First, pastors and other leaders in the church need to hold forth these principles as the agenda of the church. This is the church's business. It is the fulfillment of Jesus' great command that we "make disciples." There are so many other things people think the church should be or to which it should commit its resources. Many voices suggest that a local church determine its unique mission. But then we run the danger of neglecting or ignoring the single purpose for every church: to become the people of God through his forming and transforming power. What other mission do we need? How can we say to God that this isn't enough, that the mandate of changed lives isn't a specific enough goal? The mission has been set out. Unlike a company or corporation that can choose its mission, the church must follow a mission handed down by a higher authority. Mission is given, and it is either accepted or neglected.

We must be genuine, not glib, superficial, or falsely spiritual about transformation. We must guard our attitudes from being cliché about Christian faith in its most profound realities. Phrases such as "changed lives," "transformation," and "renewal" come easily. They sound good and right, ring out from the pulpit, and make good chapters in books and study guides. But we must not take these expressions and use them as props for church rhetoric. We must speak authentically of such things, and we should flesh out their meaning in terms of people's everyday lives. We should provide forums for people to testify to transformation in their lives because personal testimony is direct, concrete, and stops the mouths of gainsayers. To model the form or pattern of spiritual life is to promote one of the most formative experiences a person can have.

Take ceremonial events of church life as opportunities to focus on the prospect and promise of transformation. The Lord's Supper is a moment where the spotlight is on death, sacrifice, and the consequential giving of life. Baptism depicts the transformation from death and burial to life. Funerals for believers provide clear opportunities to draw out the unique hope for a metamorphosis to a higher state of being. Only at a Christian wedding ceremony can the pastor charge the bride and groom to set their sights on the ongoing process of transformation, their only hope for marital success and satisfaction.

As leaders in the church we need to keep our personal focus on transformation. What is it that we aspire to? When do we feel as though we are being "successful" in ministry? What kind of applause are we tempted to seek? The answers—good and bad—are obvious enough. A chorus of voices, without and within, call us to be shaped according to some partisan or institutional set of expectations. Those voices are not always wrong, but neither are they always right.

The apostle Paul dealt with many who wanted to shape his beliefs and behavior. His brilliant answer was full of both conviction and honesty:

> I care very little if I am judged by you or by any human court; indeed, I do not even judge myself. My conscience is clear, but that does not make me innocent. It is the Lord who judges me. Therefore judge nothing before the appointed time; wait till the Lord comes. He will bring to light what is hidden in darkness and will expose the motives of men's hearts. At that time each will receive his praise from God.
>
> 1 Corinthians 4:3–5

Notice the points Paul makes: (1) we will be judged by others; (2) the judgments of others may or may not be right; (3) we should be careful even of our judgments about ourselves; (4) we should strive for a clear conscience; (5) having a clear conscience, however, does not absolutely guarantee that we are innocent; (6) God is the only ultimate judge of our actions; (7) in this life we may not know with complete certainty whether a particular act was the right thing or not; (8) someday we will know where we did right and where wrong; and (9) at that time we will be safe and loved by God.

Think about it. How could a congregation ask for more than this in a spiritual leader—a deep and sustained commitment to seek the transformation of Christ in his or her life and to promote the same reality in the congregation. This is the focal point of Christian experience, community, and mission. We must not be distracted from it.

The dynamics of spiritual formation are, in the final analysis, the normal flow of the grace of God into the life of the Christ-follower. We are responsible, as individuals and as the church, to actively seek this grace where it may be found. But in the end, the shaping of souls is a great mystery, an act of God from beginning to end. And he does it.

Lord Jesus, as God's Spirit came down and rested on you, may the same Spirit rest upon us, bestowing his sevenfold gifts.

First, grant us the gift of understanding, by which your precepts may enlighten our minds.

Second, grant us counsel, by which we may follow in your footsteps on the path of righteousness.

Third, grant us courage, by which we may ward off the Enemy's attacks.

Fourth, grant us knowledge, by which we can distinguish good from evil.

Fifth, grant us piety, by which we may acquire compassionate hearts.

Sixth, grant us fear, by which we may draw back from evil and submit to what is good.

Seventh, grant us wisdom, that we may taste fully the life-giving sweetness of your love.

Bonaventura (1217–1274)

Appendix

What Is the "Soul"?

Every religion and every philosophy has a theory of what lies within the human person. That intangible inner self has been described with so many different words—soul, spirit, mind, will, energy, heart—and they all describe something of who we are and why we behave the way we do. Not mere idle speculation, this issue influences how we think about who the Creator is and what is his intent, how sin or corruptibility interferes with what we are supposed to be, and how we are actually saved. It shapes Christian devotion in prayer and worship.

One of the earliest Christian theologians, Tertullian of Carthage, commented,

> Look within yourself and you'll get some idea of how much the soul contains. Consider what enables you to think; ponder the abilities of the prophet. Even in a fallen condition, the soul does not forget its Creator. . . . If the knowledge of the soul comes from any written source, it would be scripture . . . What difference does it make

whether soul knowledge came from God or from his book? . . . If you believe in God and nature, then have faith in the soul. On that basis you will be able to believe in yourself.[1]

More skeptical voices from our own century aren't so sure. Lord Byron said, "One certainly has a soul; but how it came to allow itself to be enclosed in a body is more than I can imagine. I only know if once mine gets out, I'll have a bit of a tussle before I let it get in again to that of any other." Herman Melville adds: "Our souls are like those orphans whose unwedded mothers die in bearing them: the secret of our paternity lies in their grave, and we must there to learn it." And D. H. Lawrence concludes: "My soul is my great asset and my great misfortune."

What is the meaning of "soul"? What about "spirit"? What is the spiritual life? It is nonsense for us to develop a plan for spiritual formation if we do not know what it is that is being formed. Pastors, theologians, and other spiritual leaders, in trying to define spiritual life, usually find that a theoretical concept of the soul or spirit underlies and shapes their concept of devotion. Such concepts are not mere abstractions; they are how we view our inner lives and the basis for how we define salvation. Several viewpoints exist.

View #1: The Soul Is a Part of God

This dangerous viewpoint assumes that human nature is divine because the origin of the universe derives from the being of God himself. It interprets "made in God's image" to indicate derived divinity. Human beings are spiritual beings in that they are part of the Spirit. In this life it appears we are separate from

God. That is why we speak, inaccurately though naturally, about God as being separate and distinct from us. However, we are divinity, and the spiritual life is the quest to discover our real identity.

Numerous Eastern religions are based on these basically pantheistic assumptions. Yet there are also instances where extreme forms of Christian mysticism have promoted this view as the proper view of Christian spirituality. This was the case with fourteenth-century German mystic Meister Eckhart. Taking Christian mysticism to an extreme, Eckhart both gained followers and brought charges of heresy against himself by his insistence that the human soul becomes one with God.

> The being and the nature of God are mine; Jesus enters the castle of the soul; the spark in the soul is beyond time and space; the soul's light is uncreated and cannot be created, it takes possession of God with no mediation; the core of the soul and the core of God are one.[2]

In this view we must pass through several stages for the soul to have union with God. It must be seen first as dissimilar, next as similar, then as identified before the "breakthrough" where finally "the soul is above God."

Not surprisingly, such provocative statements brought charges of heresy on Eckhart's head. But it was not the first time such a view of spirituality had been raised in the Christian community. As early as the fifth century Dionysius combined Neoplatonic philosophy and Christianity to promote a type of mysticism in which the soul discovers its divine nature. His spiritual method involved the disciplined abandonment of senses leading to "light from the divine darkness" and union with God.

Medieval tradition had several Dionysian streams running through it, and down to the present day some contemporary forms of devotion continue this strong emphasis of the identity of divinity and the soul.

So thought a friend of mine who got involved with a group who taught him that worshiping, praying, and other external deeds were ridiculous for the believer who has become one with God. My friend began telling everyone he had no sin and told his fellow elders on the board at his church that he was Christ. Soon he fell away from the Christian community altogether.

Augustine spoke for all times when he warned:

> Don't ever let anyone persuade you that the soul partakes of God! To believe the soul is part of God is a terrible heresy. The worst heretics say that the soul emanated out of God. We don't even say that the Father, Son, and Holy Spirit are one and the same thing but maintain their separateness. The same is true of the soul, what you must say is that the soul comes from God as a gift, and a gift alone. . . . All creatures come from God and are not made of his nature. He created the world ex-nihilo, out of nothing. We come "out of him" only in the sense God initiates our existence.[3]

View #2: The Soul Is an Immortal Spiritual Entity

The man on the street who has just a vague remembrance of Christian belief may think of the soul as a ghostly, immaterial form that is infused in the body until death when it floats away into some ethereal existence. Unfortunately, what he is recollecting is not so much an orthodox Christian memory, but a Neoplatonic spirituality mixed up with Christian lingo that depicts "spirit" as disembodied being. Ghost stories in literature, television, and film perpetuate this idea.

It's not surprising that some of the Christian thinkers of the Greco-Roman era left a few Hellenistic foundation blocks in the new edifice of Christian theology they constructed. The dualism of body and spirit and the idea of an immortal soul—separable from the body, eternally existent, and even preexistent—were carried over in whole or in part by such thinkers as Clement of Alexandria, Origen, and even Augustine.

This view's attraction consists in the nobility and substantiality attributed to our spiritual selves. There really is a soul, and it is inherently good. Here also may be found a neat explanation for the spiritual struggle in us. The spirit or soul represents what is good and right. So it is some rude intruder (namely, the material body) that is to blame for unrighteous word and deed.

Spiritual formation, in this scenario, is the quest to submit the mischievous body to the inherent righteousness of the soul. A superficial reading of some biblical passages would support such an idea. John 6:63 says, "The Spirit gives life; the flesh counts for nothing." And in Romans 7:25 Paul claims, "I myself with my mind am serving the law of God, but on the other, with my flesh the law of sin" (NASB). Orthodox Christian teaching, however, calls the spirit/flesh dualism into question and interprets the whole of the Scriptures as saying that God is the creator of both spirit and body, that both are affected by sin, and that both are redeemable by the power and grace of God. In spiritual formation, the soul must be shaped; it is not the shaper.

View #3: The Spirit (Distinct from Soul) Is the Intersection of the Divine and the Human

Some theological anthropologies portray "spirit" as a special part of the human being that is the place of contact between God and person. "Soul," by contrast, refers to that part of our interior lives that includes the more creaturely functions of cognition, emotion, and volition. If this is the case, then spiritual formation is the task of getting the spirit to more completely control both the soul and the body.

Though traditional Christian thought has spoken of the inner life as a unity called spirit, soul, mind, or heart, occasional theologies have committed to a trichotomous view of human personhood. Apollinaris of Laodocia (c.a. 240 A.D.) proposed that a three-part view of human nature explained the person of Christ who had, in place of a human spirit, a divine nature. Not much more was said until modern times when numerous devotional sources used the view to explain the spiritual life. Proponents argue that New Testament passages that use "spirit," "soul," and "body" (e.g., 1 Thess. 5:23) portray human nature as three-fold with parallels in the Trinity.

The theory of spiritual life that proceeds from this anthropology goes as follows. Separated from God, unregenerate people are spiritually dead; their "spirits" are non-living or impotent. Salvation brings the spirit to life. This is the link to God who is himself Spirit. The challenge now is for the spirit to have control over soul and its functions (thinking, feeling, willing, etc.) and over the body and its functions. The struggle and striving for spiritual growth goes on within the human personality—God having his beachhead in the spirit of the person, and human nature firmly entrenched in the soul and in the flesh.

Proponents of this view claim this as the way of understanding human beings as genuinely spiritual creatures. It is not that the spirit is a bit of the godhead (as in the soul-as-part-of-God view), but it bears the real likeness of God and is the place of contact, the means of revelation, and the assurance of organic union with God.

The main problems with this alternative come in that the Scriptures seem to speak of spirit and soul, and, for that matter, mind, heart, and inner being, interchangeably.[4] They do not describe human nature as divisible into parts. Old and New Testament passages assume the unity of human nature, not even separating the physical self from the spiritual self as was fundamental to so many of the early religions and philosophies of the world.

View #4: "Soul" and "Spirit" Are Simply Terms for Our Collective Consciousness

Assuming a materialistic or empirical worldview, this view locates all human experience in the body, its reasoning, and emoting as functions of the brain. Cultures past and present have depicted soul or spirit in the human person because they try to describe our collective consciousness. The sum of our aspirations, fears, beliefs, values, and ideas, however, are simply the impulses of the brain or mind, as it reacts to the world around it.

One day I had a conversation about spiritual life with a modernist-minded pastor. He pointed at a rock and exclaimed, "I have as much soul as that rock." It was then that I realized why we were not connecting. We had two entirely different universes in view. I suppose he thought that it was liberating to let go of outmoded, superstitious views of life that include "soul," but I would have a hard time thinking of myself as a lump of dirt guiding other lumps of dirt to some altruistic end.

This is as much the heart of modernism as anything. David Hume told us in 1739 that the only things we can know are what our physical senses perceive. Immanuel Kant further explained that any metaphysical categories (God, soul, etc.) are ultimately unknowable. And Friedrich Schliermacher, the father of modern liberal theology, taught that religion is really just sentiment. People who accepted their views lost the need for the soul.

This evacuation of the soul left a spiritual vacuum. Many ministry practitioners in this century have filled it with Jungian psychology, viewing religions, myths, fantasies, and fairy tales as revelations of the "collective unconsciousness" that binds all humanity together. Universally inherited symbols, images, feelings, thoughts, and memories become a modern version of "soul."

Given this view of the soul, spiritual formation cannot mean any more than the progressive moral ordering of life or the authentication of the individual.

View #5: Soul or Spirit as the Divinely Created Inner Life

Classical Christian teaching most accurately reflects biblical descriptions of human beings as a divinely created unity of body and soul (or spirit) made in God's image, corrupted by sin, but capable of restoration. "Body" or "flesh" (in its simplest sense) describes the tangible, material self, while a variety of other terms (soul, spirit, mind, heart, will, etc.) depict the amazingly complex inner life given all human beings. Each word emphasizes an aspect of who we are or how we function rather than a distinguishable segment of human nature.

Term	Meaning	References
soul	the human person as animated by the living power of God	Genesis 2:7 Mark 8:35
spirit	the human person as the image of God, possessing morality, consciousness, creativity, and other God-like characteristics	1 Corinthians 2:10-16
mind	the inner life with special reference to rationality or cognition	Romans 7:25 Colossians 2:18
heart	the inner life—inclusive of thought, emotion, and volition, but with special reference to the core of the inner life	Romans 10:6, 8-10
will	the faculty of choice	Luke 22:42
body	the material self	Matthew 6:25 1 Corinthians 6:13-20
flesh	the body or human nature as limited or fallen	1 Corinthians 15:39 Ephesians 2:3 1 John 4:2-3

The Scriptures depict a human being as one person (organic unity) with two aspects (physical and spiritual) and many functions (cognition, emotion, volition, etc.). Instead of saying we have a body, or a soul, or a spirit, it would be better for us to say we are body, soul, spirit, mind, heart, etc. There is no "I," no "self," apart from these characteristics. There is no time in our days on earth when one is isolated from another.

Break your leg and you're more likely to scream "I'm hurt!" than state, "My body is hurt." You do not set up an appointment for your body to get a haircut while you send your spirit to church and your mind to the library. In worship we say, "We worship you." Lovers hear and say, "I love you." When we do want to convey the marvel of the many levels of our love or devotion or comprehension, then we use words such as mind, heart, soul, spirit—not to divide or partition ourselves, but to express fullness.

All this is not merely an academic point. How we view spiritual formation will rise directly out of how we view the human person. If we are a unity of body, soul, spirit, mind, strength, and will, then there is a tremendous fluidity between our motives, impulses, vices, and virtues. Though in our ways of speaking we sometimes distinguish thoughts, feelings, decisions, actions, and "spiritual" sensations, there are no bold lines drawn between these experiences. When I say I am "in love" with my wife, am I referring to an act of will, an emotional sentiment, an opinion, a bodily longing—or all of the above? What about conversion? Some conversions seem more intellectual (e.g., C. S. Lewis), others more emotional (e.g., John Bunyan), and still others a sea change of the will (e.g., Augustine). Yet we know that, in some way, conversion has to include all. Regarding worship, some will say they have really worshiped when their minds are raised to divine truth. Others say the same when they have felt something. Still others say so only when they walk away motivated to do something. And a few claim a special spiritual experience that is not exactly any of the above. Yet how can we say we are worshiping if we are not presenting all of who we are on bended knee before God?

Archbishop William Temple said, "We only know what matter is when spirit dwells in it; we only know what man is when God dwells in him."[5] There is no aspect of us that is either incapable of worship or more capable. God made us. He made all of us, and he is interested in nothing less than our loving him with all our "mind, heart, soul, and strength." That was Jesus' way of pointing to the whole of us—every spiritual and physical aspect.

Notes

Chapter 3: War against the Soul

1. John Wesley, *Sermons,* sermon XV in *Works of John Wesley,* A. C. Outler and Reginal Word, eds. (Nashville: Abingdon, 1988), 182.

Chapter 4: From Text to Godliness

1. John K. Ryan, ed., *The Confessions of St. Augustine* (New York: Doubleday, 1960), 202.

2. Preface to John Spangenberg's *German Postils,* quoted in Doberstein, *Ministers' Prayer Book* (Philadelphia: Fortress, 1986), 306.

3. In a letter to Gregory, quoted in Hugh Thomson Kerr, *Preaching in the Early Church* (New York: Revell, 1942), 111.

4. Quoted in Doberstein, 311.

5. *Gnomon Novi Testamenti,* 1742, quoted in Doberstein, 312.

6. *An open letter to the Christian nobility,* quoted in Doberstein, 312.

7. Quoted in Doberstein, 311.

8. Robert Mulholland, *Shaped by the Word: The Power of Scripture in Spiritual Formation* (Nashville: Upper Room, 1986), 58.

9. Ibid., 53.

10. Richard Foster and James Bryan Smith, eds., *Devotional Classics: Selected Readings for Individuals and Groups* (San Francisco: HarperCollins, 1993), 2.

11. John Wesley, *The Works of John Wesley*, 3d ed., vol. 14 (Kansas City: Beacon Hill Press, 1979), 252.

Chapter 5: Dialogue with God

1. John R. W. Stott, *Christian Basics* (Grand Rapids: Eerdmans, 1969), 118–19.

Chapter 7: To Know and to Be Known

1. Alister McGrath points out that the Protestant reformers did not object to the concept of spiritual direction as along as it is understood that every Christian stands before God with equal status. *Roots That Refresh: A Celebration of Reformation Spirituality* (London: Hodder & Stoughton, 1991), 26.

2. A. B. Hyde, *The Story of Methodism throughout the World from the Beginning to the Present Time* (Springfield, Mass., and Chicago: Wiley & Co., 1887/1888), 168–70.

3. Ibid., 171.

4. Frederick A. Norwood, *The Story of American Methodism: A History of the United Methodists and Their Relations* (Nashville: Abingdon Press, 1974), 130.

5. Ibid., 131.

Chapter 8: The Shaping Word

1. John R. W. Stott, *The Contemporary Christian* (Downers Grove, Ill.: InterVarsity Press, 1992), 174, 208.

2. D. Martyn Lloyd-Jones, *Preaching and Preachers* (Grand Rapids: Zondervan, 1971), 9.

3. Quoted in Stott, *Between Two Worlds*, 42.
4. Justin Martyr, in *Ante-Nicene Fathers*, vol. 1 (Grand Rapids, Eerdmans, 1983), 186.
5. Tertullian, in *Ante-Nicene Fathers*, vol. 3 (Grand Rapids: Eerdmans, 1983), 46.
6. Stott, *Between Two Worlds*, 145.

Chapter 9: The Expended Life

1. John Dillenberger, *Martin Luther: Selections from His Writings* (New York: Doubleday, 1961), 53.

Chapter 10: Metamorphosis

1. John Owen, *Sin and Temptation: The Challenge to Personal Godliness* (Portland, Oreg.: Multnomah, 1983), 192.
2. John Wesley, *Sermons on Several Occasions* (London: The Epworth Press, 1944), 6.
3. Richard Baxter, *The Reformed Pastor* (Edinburgh: Banner of Truth Trust, 1656),117.
4. Philip Hughes, *The True Image: The Origin and Destiny of Man in Christ* (Grand Rapids: Eerdmans, 1989), viii–ix.
5. John Chrysostom, *Commentary on St. John* (Washington, D.C.: Catholic University of America Press, 1957), 106.

Appendix: What Is the "Soul"?

1. Quoted in Robert L. Wise, *Quest for the Soul* (Nashville: Thomas Nelson, 1996), 126.
2. "Eckhart, Meister" in *Encyclopedia Britannica*, vol. 4 (1986), 351.
3. Quoted in Wise, 148.

4. Compare Matthew 20:28 with its parallel, Mark 10:45. Also see Luke 14:6 and Mark 12:30.

5. William Temple, "The Divinity of Christ," in B. H. Streeter, ed., *Foundations* (London: Macmillan, 1920), 259.

Subject Index

meaning of, 98–101
See also fellowship, formative

Laud, William, 127
Lawrence, D. H. 155
Lewis, C. S., 51, 66, 163
Lincoln, Abraham, 115
Lloyd-Jones, D. Martyn, 115
Lord's Supper, 90, 100–101
Luther, Martin, 21, 121
  on church music, 40
  on preaching, 115
  on reading, 57–58, 59
  on service, 130

Marshall, Peter, 67–68
Martyr, Justin, 116
Melville, Herman, 155
mentoring. See fellowship, formative, and spiritual direction
metamorphosis, 135–53
  assurance of, 146–47
  change as, 135–39
  implications of, for the min-
    istry of the church, 150–53
  resurrection as, 148–50
ministry, definition of, 9
Mulholland, Robert, 63–64
music, 39–41

Newton, John, 116
Norwood, Frederick, 105–6

Origen, 58, 158
Owen, John, 54–55, 137–38

Phelps, Austin, 116
prayer, formative, 67–80
  incense as image of, 68–70
  as position, 70–72
  as power, 72–73
  as presence, 72
  promoting of, in the church,
    78–80
  as purpose, 73
  solitude and, 76–78
  as spiritual awareness, 70–73

preaching, formative, 113–26
  authenticity of, 121–22
  goal of, 118–19
  as more than relevant, 124–25
  nature and importance of,
    113–18
  prospects of, 120–24
  as translation, 123–24

reading, formative, 56–66
  as divine reading (lectio div-
    ina), 62–66
  importance of, 57–60
  modeling, 60–61
  prescribing, 62

Schliermacher, Friedrich, 161
service, formative, 127–34
  biblical meaning of, 129–30
  moving people toward, 131–33
  and spiritual formation,
    133–34
  See also diakonia
shepherding
  functions of, 119
  nature of, 19
sin
  as deformation, 44–55
  vocabulary of, 49–51
  See also Owen, John; Wesley,
    John, analysis of sin
small groups. See class meetings
soul
  aiming ministry at the, 23–26
  definition of, 154–64
  as the divinely created inner
    life, 161–64
  as an immortal spiritual entity,
    157–58
  as the intersection of the divine
    and the human, 159–60
  as a part of God, 155–57
  and spirit as terms for our collec-
    tive consciousness, 160–61
spiritual development
  as growth, 30–33

as integration of the aesthetic
side of life, 39–41
as integration of our lives with
creation, 38–39
as integration of our relationships, 39
as integration of who we are,
34–38
through crisis, 41–46
See also spiritual formation;
spiritual growth
spiritual experience, types of,
26–28
spiritual formation
defined, 15–16
principles of, 20–23
See also spiritual development;
spiritual growth
spiritual growth
metaphors for, 17, 30–31
and soul shaping, 18–20
See also spiritual development;
sspiritual formation
Stott, John, 69–70, 114
on preaching, 123

Temple, William, 85, 163–64
Tertullian, 116, 154

transformation. *See* metamorphosis

Wesley, John
analysis of sin, 53–54
and class meeting, 103–4
on reading, 61–62, 65–66
on salvation, 138
transformation of, 18–19,
21–22
Willard, Dallas, 130
worship, formative, 81–95
as bowing or bending, 82–85
defining, 89
differing styles of, 87–88
effects of, 92–93
practices of, 90–92
purposes of, 88–90
as service, 85–86
steps to planning, 94–95

Zinzendorf, Nikolaus Ludwig
von, 15
Zwingli, Ulrich, 40

Scripture Index

Mel Lawrenz is the senior associate pastor at Elmbrook Church in suburban Milwaukee and also serves as the director of the Elmbrook Christian Study Center. He has degrees from Carroll College, Trinity Evangelical Divinity School, and Marquette University (Ph.D.). Among Dr. Lawrenz's books are *Why Do I Feel Like Hiding?* and *Life after Grief: How to Survive Loss and Trauma.*